PLATO'S
THE
REPUBLIC

**AND
PHAEDRUS
SYMPOSIUM
APOLOGY
CRITO
PHAEDO
AND OTHER WORKS**

LEO RAUCH
ASSISTANT PROFESSOR OF PHILOSOPHY
NEW YORK UNIVERSITY

MONARCH PRESS
A DIVISION OF SIMON & SCHUSTER, INC.
1 WEST 39th STREET
NEW YORK, NEW YORK 10018

For J., for all the good reasons.

CONTENTS

INTRODUCTION

WHAT IS PHILOSOPHY? Most philosophers believe that philosophy begins in wonder, and thus has its roots somewhere in human nature itself.

Men are probably the only creatures who can wonder. They can wonder at the "mystery of man's existence" and at the fact that the world exists or, finding no such "mysteries," can wonder about the nature of the world (whether it is material or spiritual, moving or still) and the nature of man's knowledge of it.

Out of this wonder, two men in ancient Greece created philosophy as we know it today—as the systematic investigation of the ultimate nature of reality and of man's relation to reality. If a man has ever wondered whether the world he sees around him is *really* real, he has been wondering about "the ultimate nature of reality." If he has ever asked himself, "How can I ever be sure I know anything? I've been so sure before, and been wrong then. How can I know I'm right now?" or if he has ever asked himself, "Why should I be moral?" he has been asking about his "relation to reality." Such a man has been asking philosophical questions. When he asks and answers such questions systematically, he becomes a philosopher.

(Even before philosophy came upon the scene, there must have been some Canaanite shepherds who asked questions such as: "What keeps the stars up?" and "What is the soul?" The difference between the way these questions are asked by Canaanite shepherds and Athenian philosophers is that the shepherds are idle in their questioning. It takes them nowhere. And when they cannot find an answer they give up wondering. When they do find an answer it is isolated from everything else they know.)

Can we say then what makes a great philosopher, the kind of philosopher we can read with profit today, though he wrote more than 2,000 years ago?

PLATO'S IMPORTANCE: Plato is often called "The Prince of Philosophy." There are two reasons for this title. First because he asks many of the fundamental philosophical questions, questions that are still being asked by philosophers today. These are questions such as: What is truth? What is justice? What is reality? Modern philosophers might not answer these questions in the way that Plato answered them, but it is significant that, in any case, they are giving their modern solutions to his problems. No modern composer writes music like that of Bach, but no important composer can ignore him.

The second reason for Plato's right to be called "The Prince of Philosophy" is, I think, that many of his answers have been continuously meaningful, and are still meaningful for us today. To his fundamental questions, Plato gives some of the best answers ever given. Each age rediscovers for itself Plato's persistent value. Many of our contemporary advances in logic and the theoretical side of mathematics, for example, can be traced back to Plato. Alfred N. Whitehead, a famous mathematician and logician, as well as a deep thinker on the theory of the cosmos, can say something like, "Wherever I go in my mind, I always meet Plato coming back."

Even if we disagree with Plato, as some great philosophers do, his ideas are so profound and so persuasively argued for that his opponents always have to be able to refute him. It is in these respects, therefore, that we might say that *all* of subsequent philosophy (and that includes the whole vast history of western thought, from Aristotle through the Middle Ages, through philosophy in our own time) can be accurately characterized as "a series of footnotes to Plato."

PLATO'S BACKGROUND: Socrates, the man whom Plato idealized in his writings, lived and taught in the last half of the fifth century B.C. Plato studied under him but did his writing during the first half of the fourth century B.C. In the time of Socrates, Greek values and the Greek view of life were being attacked in a powerful way. In the time of Plato, those values were already dead: the Golden Age of Greek democracy was finished. It has been said that philosophy arises only when a culture finds its values threatened or when the culture itself is dying. "The owl of Minerva takes to flight only when the darkness has fallen," says the German nineteenth-century philosopher, Hegel. He is speaking of Socrates. The Athenian Empire was in its death-throes, and people were asking themselves what it is that could really be believed. Evidently, the values they had trusted could be trusted no longer, for if they were true, why hadn't they worked? What Socrates tried to do, therefore, was to establish such concepts as truth, justice, and reality, on a soberly rational and scientific basis, quite independently of all inherited traditions.

PLATO FOR OURSELVES: It is easy to find, in all this, many direct applications for our own time. We, too, live in a time when our values are under attack. We no longer trust our values in the same way that our forefathers did.

(1) In political philosophy they could speak of truths which they held to be "self-evident," namely that all men were created equal and endowed by their creator with certain inalienable rights. Some modern theorists want to retain such a concept as "rights," but they do not necessarily want them to be dependent upon the actions of a creator. Other theorists attack the concept of a "right" if we take it to mean a "natural law" embedded in the very cosmos itself. Still others want to rule out the concept of "rights" and replace it with a concept of certain procedural advantages to be gained by acting "as if" men had rights. "Rights," in other words, are not as "self-evident" as they were once taken to be.

(2) In addition, modern science has completely overturned our picture of reality. When we can theorize about such peculiar sub-atomic particles as neutrinos that have no mass, only velocity (that is, they cannot be collected in a container, because as soon as you stop their motion they go out of existence), our trust in our own sense of a solid, stable reality may be shaken to its foundations. Now, when we combine our modern distrust in our traditional political values with our distrust for our ordinary interpretation of reality, we can see that our age is one in which many people no longer place the usual reliability in our grasp of things. It is an age of "humiliated thought," as the modern French writer, Albert Camus, says.

Our problem, therefore, consists of a re-evaluation of values and a re-interpretation of reality. This same two-fold problem was faced by Plato. I have already mentioned Socrates' (and Plato's) attempt to establish political values on a rational and scientific basis. If, as the Greeks saw, other peoples held their own values with the same kind of conviction with which the Greeks held theirs, and even Greek values were undergoing change, then what values were real?

And the physical world, as well, came in for a drastic re-interpretation. Two earlier writers, Parmenides and Heraclitus, had views that directly contradicted one another. Heraclitus held that all reality is undergoing constant change. Parmenides held that only what is unchanging is real; the world of our changing experience is therefore illusory. Plato resolves the conflict by showing that there is a gradation of realities, wherein the highest is the unchanging, and the lowest is the world of images, mirages, and changing illusions. The difference between Plato's view and that of the earlier thinkers is that Plato has a more highly sophisticated theory of meaning, a theory in which words refer to the most real things, the pure forms or ideas —and these forms are, of course, more real than any concrete aspect of the world itself.

As to the re-evaluation of values, Plato's attempt to establish these on a scientific basis requires us to ask whether a science of man (such as a science of politics or psychology) is at all possible. If, as we just saw, the world of change is an illusory world, and man is part of that illusory, changing world, then it would appear that a true science of man is impossible. Plato, however, will not leave it at that. He wants to find the conditions that actually make a human science possible. One of the most searching questions he asks, therefore, is, "How is a human science possible?" When Plato uses the word "science" he means something like mathematics, with its unchanging truths. Can there be such a science of man, a science that would give us absolute certainty, despite the facts of human change?

Thus, we find that our own re-evaluation of our culture's values and our re-interpretation of reality are foreshadowed by Plato's own problem: the problem of change. If cultural values change, what values are real? If the physical world is always changing, then what aspect of "reality" is real?

COMMENT: Plato has something to say about some other

contemporary issues. (1) Many of the questions that are now being discussed by philosophers and psychologists were discussed first by Plato. The modern school of psychology known as Behaviorism finds itself confronted by "new" questions that received their most probing analysis by Plato. Is consciousness a brain-process? Is psychological behavior basically different from physical behavior? If there is no basic difference, does this mean that psychology is ultimately reducible to physiology and physics? Can psychological descriptions be translated into physiological descriptions?

This is a cluster of questions which carries the title of the "Mind-Body Problem." Behaviorism and its philosophical foundation (Physicalism) form one set of answers to the problem: "mind" is reduced to "body"; there is only one kind of reality and it is physical. This might appear as the most obvious position to take. Yet is is a position that is riddled with difficulties, and it does not necessarily make for simplicity. Another way of approaching the problem is to retain the two-fold reality of mind and body. This view, a dualism, has also had its due treatment at the hands of Plato.

Some philosophers have tried to dismiss the problem as nothing but a question of semantics. Nevertheless, the problem comes back. Although it has not been resolved (and is perhaps insoluble), we must continue to ask these questions. The asking helps us turn up new insights into human nature—even though the problem persists as unsolved. The reason why we go back to Plato is that we might gain a fresh perspective and then start all over.

(2) Another broad area of concern in which Plato is being read is that of political theory. We may *feel* that democracy is the best form of government. But is this conviction of ours something which we can also establish theoretically? If we want to think of ourselves as complete human beings, functioning on all levels, then the feeling alone cannot suffice. Emotion cannot do the work of intellect. We have all seen the dangers involved when that sort of thing has been tried: vast crowds shouting, "Heil!"

Now, Plato thought that democracy is tragically inadequate as a form of government. He had excellent evidence for his view: Athens had been defeated after a long and deadly war. There is no question but that the democracy contributed to its own defeat. This is not, however, the substance of Plato's indictment of democracy. His case is far more challenging—as we shall see. Perhaps, then, if we can withstand Plato's attack we can find new "reasons," new intellectual grounds for what we already hold true on the basis of feeling and loyalty and tradition.

(3) What Plato and philosophy ask of us, then, is that we put our beliefs on the line, and follow our thoughts no matter where they might lead. This is a kind of passion. After all, what intellectual passion and erotic passion have in common is the inescapable need to pursue an object to its conclusion—whether that object be an idea or a person. In this light, Plato is one of the most courageous and passionate of philosophers.

If we can rationally justify what we believe, then well and good. If we cannot, however, then we must bravely surrender our hold on our beliefs, and believe only that which we can satisfactorily prove to ourselves. This can be a very frightening prospect to many people. It is not every day that we are asked to show grounds for our beliefs or else give them up, to agree to defend them successfully (and Plato would make a powerful adversary) or else to run from the field of battle. Imagine what it would be, had we to do this as a way of life.

Socrates and Plato did, however, choose this as a way of life: endless questioning, taking hold of one's beliefs and weighing them once again, each day. This choice had different consequences for each. For Socrates, the result was that he was condemned to death for doing just this— and we shall see how he freely chooses death rather than give up the pursuit of what his mind has shown him. (Perhaps, then, Erasmus is right, and there is enough nobility in this martyrdom for proper sainthood.) For Plato, the result was that he founded the first university in the world.

Something must be said now about the personal character of these two men, of their relation to one another, and of the time in which they lived. Let us begin, however, with a mystery.

THE SOCRATIC MYSTERY: Socrates, we know, never wrote a word. Practically all that we know of him is what we can gather from Plato's descriptions of him in the *Dialogues*. (A book of reminiscences of Socrates by Xenophon, *Memorabilia*, some fragments from dialogues by Aeschines, and the lampoon of Socrates by Aristophanes in *The Clouds* contribute little to our picture of Socrates.) Our mystery is this: Is Plato presenting Socrates as he really was, as expressing ideas which were really his? Or is Plato using Socrates merely as a dramatic figure, a spokesman for views he never held? Is the Socrates of Plato's *Dialogues* uttering the philosophy of Socrates or the philosophy of Plato? There are two schools of thinking about this problem.

THE ENGLISH VIEW: Plato's representation of Socrates has to be a faithful one. The character in the *Dialogues* could not be a mere persona for the views of Plato, since the *Dialogues* were meant to be read and heard by people who had known Socrates well. Any deliberate mis-characterization would have been pointless—as pointless as writing a book called "Chats with Churchill" in which Churchill is represented as saying, "I always felt that a German victory would be the best thing for the world."

THE GERMAN VIEW: The character of Socrates must be a construction of Plato's to some extent since some of the *Dialogues* (such as *Protagoras*) present Socrates as a relatively young man, long before Plato was born. Other dialogues (such as *Symposium*) present Socrates in conversations which Plato was too young to have heard. Moreover, there is a significant change in some of the views of Socrates between Plato's earlier and later works. Nor does this reflect a change in the actual Socrates, since some of the earlier *Dialogues* present an elderly Socrates, but with Plato's early views!

There is much to be said for either school, and as yet neither argument has been found to be conclusive. We know, of course, that Plato did not know Socrates for the greater part of Socrates' life. Socrates was 42 when Plato was born, Plato was 28 when Socrates died. Although it is quite likely that Plato, in his childhood, knew Socrates, certainly their contact as teacher

and disciple could not have extended much over ten years—
from the time when Plato was 18 and Socrates 60 to the time
when Plato was 28 and Socrates 70. Thus, Plato could not
have known Socrates during the crucial years of Socrates' intellectual development (which Plato has Socrates describe in
Phaedo). Nor is it likely that Plato could have heard merely
verbal accounts—remember that the *Republic* is some 400
pages long—of *actual* conversations that took place twenty
years before, and transcribed them verbatim. So there must
have been some construction. And yet, there is probably a considerable fidelity (in principle, at least) to the historical
Socrates.

What has complicated the picture is Plato's statement in his
Seventh Letter that his written *Dialogues* do not represent his
real thinking. "There neither is nor ever will be a treatise of
mine on the subject." Then, as far as Plato is concerned, the
Dialogues represent the "discourses of Socrates."

SOCRATES THE MAN: We know that he was born in or
before the year 469 B.C. and earned a very poor living as a
stonemason and carver. We also know, from the *Symposium*,
that he was short, fat, bald, with protuberant eyes and a snub-
nose, yet with great charm and self-control. He always walked
barefoot, even when standing on guard duty in the snow. He
had a fantastic ability to hold his liquor: after the all-night bout
of talk and drink described in *Symposium*, everybody is dead-
drunk except Socrates, Aristophanes, and Agathon. When dawn
comes, these last two fall asleep, but Socrates goes off to the
baths, ready for a new day.

His control of his senses extended also to his power to resist
the homosexual advances of Alcibiades. In an age when
homosexuality was commonplace, and Alcibiades is considered
the most irresistible of the lot, this is no small accomplishment
of Socrates. If all this is a fabrication of Plato's, then Plato has
given us a picture not of an other-worldly ascetic, but of a
flesh-and-bone moral athlete. In addition to his sensory and
moral power, there is his great physical power and his bravery
in the battle of Potidea. He is a very virile man who, at the
time of his death, at seventy years of age, had recently sired an
infant.

SOCRATES' PURPOSE: This man embarks upon a very dangerous mission: he will question his fellow citizens to see what

they know and believe; he will tell them what is wrong with them; he will admonish them when they are not being true to themselves. This, he feels, is a mission imposed upon him by the gods. It is divine work he is doing, and he will not set it aside even when he has to choose between it and his life.

SOCRATES' STYLE: His style in pursuing this mission is two-fold. First, he often adopts a tone of irony. This trait of his has become so famous that we often hear people characterize an attitude of someone else as "Socratic irony." It is an attitude of subtle mock humility, by which you convince your opponent that you are humble and know nothing; and in his efforts to enlighten you, he hangs himself.

Second, there is his technique of intellectual midwifery. He helps individuals to give birth to thoughts they already have within them. He puts no thoughts into the minds of the people he speaks with. "Like a midwife, I am barren myself," he says, "I have no wisdom in me."

SOCRATES' SIGN: Socrates had, in addition to his superb rationality, much of the character of the visionary and mystic. He spoke of having within him, ever since childhood, a "supernatural sign"—a voice that he heard only to forbid, never to command. In addition, Socrates was given to peculiar seizures that have now been diagnosed as a form of catalepsy. He would suddenly halt whatever he was doing and stand motionless, sometimes for an entire day. In the eyes of the Greeks, this meant that the gods had possession of him for the time. Socrates also made frequent use of the language characteristic of mystic states of consciousness.

THE SOPHISTS: These were professional teachers who travelled from city to city, giving instruction for a fee. They taught a variety of subjects, from public speaking to business administration, to naval strategy, to literary criticism, to something like an adult extension course in "How to Live the Good Life: beginners, intermediate, and advanced."

All the Sophists travelled a great deal, and this exposed them to many different ways of life. Their characteristic point of view, if they can be considered to share one, was that of Relativism: that which is a virtue in this city is a vice elsewhere; there are no absolute standards of right and wrong.

The most famous of the Sophists is Protagoras (with whom Socrates holds a conversation in Plato's dialogue called *Protagoras*. His view is that "Man is the measure of all things . . . ." By this he means that individual men are their own judge of what is good or bad for them.

> **COMMENT:** Do human standards reflect an underlying nature of man, or is everything a matter of custom and convention? In Herodotus' book *The Persian Wars*, King Darius asked some Greeks how much money they would take to eat the bodies of their fathers when they died. The Greeks were outraged at the idea. Then Darius asked certain men of India, who eat the bodies of their fathers when they die, how much money they would take to burn the bodies of their fathers, as the Greeks do. The Indians were outraged at the idea. Herodotus concludes, "Custom is king . . . ."
>
> This view is typical of the Sophists. But it implies that no absolute science of man is possible. Socrates felt that in order for human sciences (e.g., psychology, sociology) to be possible, all Relativism must be attacked, and he entered into vigorous combat with the Sophists. Socrates is diametrically opposed to the Sophists' Relativism: Socrates is an Absolutist, since he holds that there are absolute truths (as in mathematics), that ethical values are special cases of such truths, and that we can know these absolute values just as we can know these absolute mathematical truths.

THE TRIAL OF SOCRATES: After the war between Athens and Sparta had been lost, Athenians looked for someone to blame for their defeat. They turned against these intellectuals who, they felt, had undermined the moral standards and the loyalties of the young with their Relativism. None of the Sophists was Athenian, however, so they could not be prosecuted. Athens turned and condemned Socrates, as being one of these intellectuals. It is cruelly ironic, that this man, who had opposed the Sophists all his life, was now condemned to death for being one of them. (The trial is discussed in the *Apology*, below.) It is enough, for now, to say that Socrates had, by his endless questions, made enemies of some powerful men—among them some personages equivalent to what we would call advisors to Presidents and five-star generals.

In 399 B.C., Socrates was tried and found guilty of, among other things, corrupting the young (intellectually, that is). Plato states, in the *Apology*, that he (Plato) was present at the trial. At the death-scene (described in the *Phaedo*), one of the characters says that Plato could not be there because he was ill. It is easy to imagine what kind of illness could have kept him away from his friend and teacher during the last hours of his life on earth: it could only have been a profound emotional collapse. Despite his absence, however, the picture which Plato gives us of the serene courage of Socrates is one of the most memorable in all literature.

PLATO THE MAN: Of Plato's personal life we know very little. (*He* had no Plato to describe him.) We know that he was born in 427 B.C. and that he died in 347 B.C. We know something of his family because Plato himself describes them. Two of the main characters in the *Republic*, Adeimantus and Glaucon, were Plato's elder brothers. It was an aristocratic family, and the brilliant Plato was obviously destined for high government office. Two things changed his mind.

The first factor was that two of Plato's uncles, Critias and Charmides, were prominent members of a junta that took over the government. It appeared that the young Plato was being groomed to take his eventual place in this. But the government resorted to violence and lawlessness, and Plato wanted no part of it. Eventually, the democracy was restored.

The second factor is the execution of Socrates at the hands of the democracy. Plato became completely disillusioned about government in general and about democracies in particular. We shall see how, in the *Republic*, he characterizes democracy as rule by opinion, and maintains that there are some areas in which mere opinion cannot count for much. If one of us collapses, we send for a doctor—a man who knows. We do not decide democratically, by a show of hands, whether we ought to leave the victim lying on the floor or put him in a chair, give him something to drink or give him nothing, etc. If one of us does know something about first-aid, it is knowledge derived directly or indirectly from doctors. It is real knowledge that is needed here, and a mere opinion can be fatal. (It was a show of hands, after all, that had condemned Socrates.)

DEMOCRACY AND AMATEURISM: When the Athenians talked

about equality, they took it literally: every free man was the equal of every other, and this meant that every man could do the work of every other. Magistrates and many other public servants were chosen by lot. The vote was considered by many Athenians to be too discriminatory and undemocratic. The lot, however, chose men in a way that gave no preferential consideration to talent or training.

Consider what it means, today, to become a judge: years of law-school, practice before the bar, political maneuvering, etc. Athenians, however, chose their judges for the day, indiscriminately, as we choose our juries. Every man got his turn to serve in the Assembly. Generals could be (and were) elected or deposed by popular vote, from one day to the next. This contributed to the disastrous Athenian defeat. For Plato, the only solution to the ills of society is rule by experts, rule by those who know what they are doing.

AFTER THE DEATH OF SOCRATES: From 399 B.C. to 387 B.C., that is, from the age of 28 to 40 Plato travelled. He visited Italy and Sicily, and possibly Egypt and North Africa. He also wrote most of the *Dialogues* during this period. At the age of 40, after returning from Sicily, he decided to open the first institution dedicated to intensive scientific research, one of the most important events in the history of science.

THE ACADEMY: It derives its name from the fact that it was situated in an area outside Athens, sacred to the hero Academus. It had a continuous existence for over 900 years, until, in 529 A.D., the Emperor Justinian closed all schools of philosophy.

Plato was now a college president and teacher, with little time for writing. He did give lectures, but most of the "academic" activity centered around actual research.

The core of studies at the Academy was mathematics. Indeed, there is a tradition which says that Plato had a sign over the front door that read: "Let no one ignorant of geometry enter." This is perfectly characteristic, since Plato and Socrates considered it possible (and even necessary) to determine our ethical and political knowledge with the same degree of exactness as mathematics. Indeed, the *Republic* can be considered an attempt to do just this. For Plato, the model of what a science should be is mathematics. If there is to be such a thing as a social science, either it must have scientific (i.e., mathematical) certitude or else it is no science.

Soon, Plato led the Academy into the study of political theory. The Academy then came to be consulted in political matters relating to the formulation of constitutions for new colonies. Thus, Plato found that he was more important to the world than he could have been if he had stayed in the political arena of Athens.

THE GOALS OF THE ACADEMY: What the Academy sought was an Absolutist science of man, a science of values as eternal as mathematical formulae. In reply to Protagoras' view that everything is a matter of *convention*, Plato seeks to show that we can have knowledge only of things that have an eternal *nature*—whether that nature is that of man, of the cosmos, or of mathematics. In response to the Relativist principle of Protagoras that "Man is the measure of all things . . ." Plato gives an Absolutist answer, in his last work, the *Laws*, that "God is the measure of all things . . . ."

PLATO'S LATER LIFE: In 367 B.C., at the age of 60 (having been for 20 years too busy to write), Plato began writing again. The *Theaetetus* and many other important works date from this period. But his work was to be interrupted.

Twenty years before, while travelling in Sicily, Plato had made the acquaintance of the ruling house of Syracuse, the largest Greek-speaking city after Athens. Now, in 367 B.C., the old tyrant had died, and his son, Dionysius II, succeeded him. This was a thoroughly depraved individual, quite powerless to rule himself, let alone a kingdom. Meanwhile, however, the Carthaginians were invading Sicily, and all of western Hellenic civilization was in danger. What was needed was a strong monarch to unite the Greek-speaking cities of Sicily. But how could this sensualist be turned into a ruler? His brother-in-law, Dion, was a good friend of Plato and wrote him, asking the old professor to come and teach this man how to rule. At first, Plato refused. But he could not refuse for long: Plato and Dionysius, together, might create something like that union of wisdom and power of which Plato had spoken so often.

He agreed. Leaving the Academy, he made the sea voyage to Syracuse. When he got there, he found Dionysius incapable of studying anything, let alone political theory. How do you teach a man to study at all, when he has never done anything like it in his life? Well, he must get some sort of mental discipline, to begin with. Plato decided to start him on geometry. It would give him some idea of what it is to draw a conclusion. Plato demonstrated a few theorems. The King was titillated by all this, and for a time geometry was all the rage at court. But the King had no staying power for this sort of thing, and soon grew bored and Plato gave up and returned home.

Six years later, in 361 B.C., with the Carthaginians getting stronger, Dion appealed to Plato once more. The King had agreed to any sort of discipline the professor might impose. The need had been impressed upon the King, this time. Plato made another trip. His stay was even shorter, and he left Syracuse in disgust, completely fed up with politics, and returned to the Academy.

He went back to his work. Writing his last work, the *Laws,* Plato has far less hope for man than he had in the youthfully optimistic *Republic*. It is an ironic close. He died at 80, full of years, loved by his students, grandnieces and nephews.

THE REPUBLIC, BOOK I

The ostensible theme of the work is the nature of justice. But this is only a start for the discussion of a wealth of problems. Many arguments will seem to be pointlessly meandering but they are there for a reason. Plato means to give us the widest variety of detail, and to avoid mere skeletal simplicity. We shall see that the people speaking with Socrates have the illusion that they can define these ideas simply and theoretically: "Justice is nothing but . . .," and so on. They each breeze in with their theoretical convictions, all removed from life. Then Socrates shows that rules and theories can be used to save us from the effort of thinking, from making sure that they account for *all* the facts, and that we are fools if we expect such rules to relieve us of the burden of using our intelligence, or to ease us out of feeling responsible for our decisions. Life is complex, however, and theory is no substitute for it. The speakers other than Socrates see these problems as naively as though justice involved nothing more complicated than obeying traffic-lights. Naturally, once Socrates gets into his proper depth, later on, these others are reduced to contributions of "Yes, I see," and "Of course."

A word about the mechanics of the book. The numbers refer to the pagination in the edition of Stephanus (1573). These numbers are usually printed in the margins of most editions today. The pages are also divided into five segments, A to E, to make it easier to find specific sentences, but the letters are not supplied in all cases.

The persons in the dialogue are Socrates, who is also the narrator; Glaucon and Adeimantus, the brothers of Plato; Cephalus, a rich old man; Polemarchus, his son; Thrasymachus, a Sophist; and Cleitophon. The scene is the house of Cephalus at Piraeus, which is the port of Athens, about four miles from the center of the city. The time of the conversation has been estimated (from the internal evidence) to be about 421 B.C.

THE CONVERSATION: The conversation begins, casually, between Socrates and Cephalus. Socrates asks the old man whether life is harder toward the end. Cephalus answers that although others may complain of the fact that pleasures are gone, he feels that he has at last escaped a "mad and furious master." Now there is calm and freedom. The complaints one often hears, he says, stem from the character of the complainers, not from old age as such. Of course, this is easy for Cephalus to say, who is comfortable and rich. Yes, he is glad to be rich. But there are things which money cannot buy: inner peace, for example. What, then, is the greatest blessing your money *can* buy you? Socrates asks (330 D). The answer is this: a good man, if he is also rich, has no need to deceive or defraud others. He can afford to lead a life of justice, so he can make the journey to the other world with no apprehensions, no guilt.

We can feel Socrates cocking his ears at the word "justice." What is justice, actually? Is it nothing more than telling the truth and paying your debts? Surely, there are exceptions.

> **COMMENT:** Socrates is always opposed to a rule or definition that can be applied mechanically, without discernment. In this light, the Ten Commandments as well as the directives in the Sermon on the Mount would have Socrates' disapproval—merely because in their simplicity they fail to account for exceptions.

EXCEPTIONS: Let us assume that justice means telling truth and paying debts. If a man has lent me something, I owe it to him. This is a debt, an obligation on me. But suppose that what he lent me are weapons, and now he has suddenly gone crazy and wants his weapons back. Do I still owe them to him? (If I gave them to him, would I not be an accessory to whatever crime he is likely to commit?) Further, let us assume that it is right to tell the truth. That, too, is an obligation on me. But is truth-telling to such a madman a good thing to do? Suppose that he asks me, with a murderous look, whether I have seen our friend. . . . Doesn't such Kantian "rule-directed" behavior have its dangers, then?

POLEMARCHUS TAKES UP THE ARGUMENT: At the smell of an intellectual discussion, Cephalus excuses himself and leaves. One gets the feeling that he has heard all this before, and a little of it is more than enough. Life is much too short, especially now. He goes off to attend to the sacrifices, perfect behavior for an old man with his eye on the hereafter. His son, Polemarchus, takes over the argument.

The question was (331 E): Is justice the repayment of debt, pure and simple? Is it nothing more than giving every man what is coming to him? We saw that the case of the madman was an exception; we had to exercise our intelligence. But we must always do this, since we can never know anything if we don't. Polemarchus then tries to make another definition, one that will include the exception. (It is easy enough to do this: "One ought always to obey traffic lights, except when one is rushing an expectant mother to the hospital." This is now a rule.) Returning the weapons to the madman would be harmful to him, and doing harm cannot be said to be repayment. Friends ought to do good, not evil, to friends. Does that mean we ought to do evil to our enemies? Yes, that is the debt we owe our enemies, Polemarchus says.

> **COMMENT:**   Polemarchus is trying to give us rules and definitions that work without our having to think, like the sort of thing we find inscribed over a courthouse: "Justice is the giving to each man his proper due . . . ." Socrates will now try to determine the actual principles involved in the things men do, thereby getting at the underlying principles of their actions. For Polemarchus, justice is obedience to some kind of principle. For Socrates, justice involves an act of evaluation. We shall meet this concept again in the *Protagoras*: "All virtue is knowledge."

SOCRATES' EXAMPLES (332 C):   There is a series of analogies, typical of the way Socrates spins out an argument so that he may have time to think. What does the physician do? and the pilot at sea? If the art of medicine dispenses drugs, and the art of cooking dispenses food, what does the art of justice dispense? Or is justice an art of acquiring, rather than of dispensing? If, in farming we acquire corn, and in shoemaking shoes, what do we acquire by means of justice? It was said that justice involves doing good and evil. But when a man is healthy there is no need of doctors, and when we are at peace there is no need for the military. These arts are useless at least some of the time. Could it be that justice, being of two parts (good and evil, to friends and enemies, respectively), has one half that is useless part of the time? Of what use is justice, then, in its "peacetime" role, that is, when there are no friends or enemies around?

Polemarchus (333 B) pretends to answer like a businessman: justice is useful in making contracts. Any real businessman would laugh at this: the primary requirement in business is skill, not justice. In constructing a skyscraper, would the just man be a better associate than a builder? No, what we want is a man who *knows* his business.

Polemarchus retreats and tries another path: Justice is useful when you want to leave valuables with someone for safekeeping. But this means that justice is not concerned with the use of objects but with their uselessness, which means that justice is not good for much. Also, must not a good "keeper" anticipate what thieves might do? Must he not have something of the "taker" in him?

> **COMMENT:** What Socrates is aiming at is the insight that such "definitions" always have a two-fold aspect that destroys them. Viz., the absurd conclusion that every good banker, in order to be just, must also be a good thief. Justice is an art of theft. Polemarchus admits this to be absurd.

Socrates (334 C) tries once more to find the points which we must include in our definition, points not included when we follow rules blindly. We said that justice means doing good to friends, evil to enemies. Do we not have to decide, beforehand, who our friends are and who our enemies? And couldn't we be wrong? If so, we would then be doing evil to people who are really good. This cannot be justice. And suppose friends of ours are evil, and we do them good, is that justice? No, the principle works only if every one of our friends (the people to whom we do good) is a good person, and every one of our enemies is evil.

JUSTICE IS EVIL: The definition of justice involves the doing of evil to bad men and to our enemies. But animals, like dogs and horses, become worse when we harm them. By doing evil to those evil men, are we not adding to their evil, making them more evil? It follows that justice involves the actual creation of evil. Yet no art can deliberately *aim* at a negative result. The death of a patient is not a triumph of medicine but a failure. The creation of evil is not an accomplishment of justice, but a failure of justice. (335 E) (Some theorists of penology say that prisons rehabilitate, i.e., do good for inmates. Since many crimes are committed by ex-prison inmates, the evidence does not support this thesis.) But if this theory of justice—doing good to friends, evil to enemies—breaks down, what else is there?

THRASYMACHUS ENTERS (336 B): Like all Sophists, Thrasymachus prides himself on his skill in argument. But he makes a worse mistake than Polemarchus by giving a mere definition, a naive one, at that, and to this he adds rage. Socrates will destroy him on both counts. Socrates' description ("We were quite panic-stricken at the sight of him") is, of course, an excellent example of his irony.

Thrasymachus says that none of this hair-splitting will do for him. None of this business of equating justice with duty or advantage or profit, etc. He demands clearness and accuracy, he says. (What he actually wants is the simple rule which will spare him the effort of thinking.) Justice, he says, is nothing but the interest of the stronger (338 C). There are different kinds of governments: tyrannies, democracies, aristocracies. Each defines justice in its own way, and always for its own interest.

> **COMMENT:** This is Relativism with a vengeance. We might put this idea in Sophistic fashion: strength is the measure of all things. Thrasymachus believes in the amorality of politics: politics has nothing to do with ethi-

cal considerations. The strong do what they please, the weak suffer what they must. (For a particularly murderous application of this philosophy by the Athenians themselves, see Thucydides' book about the war between Athens and Sparta, *The Peloponnesian War*, Bk. V, Ch. 17. This is the famous "Melian Dialogue," in which the powerful Athenians—using the same sort of argument that Thrasymachus does—explain to the representatives of the tiny island of Melos, pleading for neutrality, that it is simply the power of Athens that forces Athens to adopt the policy that might makes right. When the Melians refused to join the Athenian alliance, the Athenians massacred all the men of Melos and sold the women and children into slavery. It is easy to imagine the "justification" that could be given by Thrasymachus for this. The conversation of the *Republic* took place around that time; Plato must have heard many such "justifications" of naked power.) Of course, Thrasymachus presents his argument for the amorality of politics as well as his defense (here in Book I of the *Republic*) quite badly. It is left for Glaucon to make a better case for the amorality of politics, later on. Plato and Socrates hold a view that is the exact opposite: ethics and politics are the same. The latter is a magnification of the former. What is justice in the individual (ethics) is the same as what is justice in the state (politics). Much modern theory has separated ethics from politics. "Render unto Caesar that which is Caesar's; render unto God that which is God's." But there also are attempts to re-unify ethics and politics, in the works of John Locke, Thomas Jefferson and John Dewey, though in senses entirely different from that of Socrates and Plato.

SOCRATES' REJOINDER TO THRASYMACHUS (339 B):
Socrates objects to the premise that justice is the interest of the stronger. He points out that a law-maker might be in error as to what is in the interests of the government. Would it be justice to obey, then? The error of Thrasymachus is the same as Polemarchus: his definition, in its simplicity, rules out certain facts. It demands mere obedience, for if we start to think about it, to test it by applying it to reality, we will find that it is false. If justice is the interest of the stronger, then what if the strong man is in error as to what is in his own interest? Wouldn't it be injustice to obey him? (Suppose that Hitler says, "Obey me because my commands are in the interests of a greater Germany."

If I feel that Hitler is wrong, and that his laws are destructive of German interests, it would be wrong for me to obey.)

Thrasymachus had said (a) that justice is simple obedience to all commands, and (b) that justice is the interest of the stronger. We now find a conflict between these two views. But for Thrasymachus there is no conflict. If the strong man is mistaken about his true interest he is not a proper strong man— any more than the physician is a proper physician when he fails. This leads us into a definition of the proper task of the ruler, a "first-draft" of which is now given by Socrates.

WHEN IS A RULER A REAL RULER?:   What is his real "interest?" A physician makes money, but we do not define medicine as the art of money-making. The same goes for other skills. The primary aim is the perfection of their practice. The true physician is first a healer, and only indirectly a maker of money. Each art is concerned with its *object* primarily and with its practitioner only secondarily. It would follow that justice is the interest of the subject, not the interest of the ruler. A real ruler is one who is primarily good for his subjects, not one who is good for himself.

THRASYMACHUS REPLIES (343 A):   After resorting to abuse, Thrasymachus points out that the shepherd fattens his flock for *his* interest, not for the sake of the flock. If you want a model of the ruler-subject relationship, don't speak of physicians and patients but of shepherds and sheep.

THE ADVANTAGES OF INJUSTICE: Thrasymachus also asks us to weigh the advantages and disadvantages of injustice as against justice: the just man is always the loser, the unjust man the gainer. Thrasymachus cites the example of an income tax: who has more to gain, the just or the unjust man? And in tyranny, which is the highest form of injustice, the greater the crime a tyrant commits, the greater his gain, not only in power but also in honor and respect.

WHAT SOCRATES MUST PROVE: What Socrates will have to show, therefore, is that justice is to be preferred over injustice —both on an individual psychological basis as well as on the larger political basis. First, we can begin by introducing a qualification into what was said earlier. True, the shepherd fattens his sheep for his own interest, yet the actual art of animal husbandry concerns the interests of the animals. When we speak of a "good herdsman" or "good doctor" we do not mean one who is financially successful, since it is possible for us to speak of a financially successful individual who is rotten as a practitioner of his art. (This serves to refine the earlier argument of Socrates to the effect that the art of ruling consists in the care of the subjects—and that any advantages to the ruler must be secondary when we speak of the art itself.)

Further, Socrates will show that the tyrant is a corruption of a natural form, a sociological cripple. If we want to know what is natural for man, it is pointless to speak of cripples since they are not typical men. One of the aims of the *Republic* as a whole will be to show that it is in the *nature* of man to be just —and to describe the kind of society in which such *natural* justice could manifest itself (even though such a society is an ideal one, not a blueprint for creating an actual state).

JUSTICE AND INJUSTICE AS WAYS OF LIFE (348 A): Obviously, if we praise injustice, as Thrasymachus does, then justice is not "the thing to do," and so we cannot identify justice as a virtue. Is justice a vice, then? No, Thrasymachus answers, it is merely sublime simplicity—a benign foolishness. Then what is injustice? It is a kind of discretion, Thrasymachus says. Those who are perfectly unjust—that is, those who get away with it— they are the smart ones, they are the wise. Justice is a fool's game. The just man might *consider* himself superior to the unjust man, Thrasymachus says (349 C), but the unjust man *is* superior to *all* men. This is a decisive difference between them: the just man is modest, the unjust superior.

SOCRATES' FINAL DEMOLITION OF THRASYMACHUS (349 E): When a skilled musician tunes a string on an instrument, does he turn the peg farther than what any skilled musician would deem proper? Obviously not. Is a physician better if he prescribes double dosages? Obviously not. In practicing a skill, we do not aim to go beyond, but only to hit the right point. Virtue is a kind of skill, and this requires a knowledge of what is the right measure. The unjust man, therefore, is not exercising much of a skill, is he? Nor is the tyrant doing much of a job at ruling. One cannot claim to play a higher F-sharp than anyone else—since we all know that F-sharp is F-sharp, and there cannot be higher or lower F-sharp's. It is the just man who knows the proper note; it is the unjust man who exceeds it and goes out of tune in his life. It is injustice, then, that is the fool's game. It destroys individuals, as it destroys states.

This, then—the physchological basis of justice (the soul in proper tune), as well as the political basis of justice (the state in proper tune)—is the theme for the remainder of the *Republic*.

THE REPUBLIC, BOOK II

Glaucon takes up the argument on behalf of the defeated Thrasymachus. But Glaucon will improve the argument by introducing certain clarifications. Good things come in three kinds: (a) goods welcome for themselves, independent of consequences; (b) goods welcome for themselves, and also for their consequences; (c) goods welcome not for themselves, but only for their consequences.

> **COMMENT:** An example of (a) would be the pursuit of happiness; of (b), sex with a view to procreation; of (c), having a tooth pulled. In modern parlance, we would call (a) an intrinsic good, (c) an instrumental good (good *for* something) and (b) a combination of (a) and (c).

In which class is justice? Glaucon asks. Socrates puts justice in (b), which he calls the highest class. Justice is desirable for its own sake as well as for its consequences. Thrasymachus had put it in (c): justice is pursued only for the sake of its consequences in rewards and reputation. No man would be just if he did not have to be.

GLAUCON'S AIM (358 B):   Glaucon wants to know what justice and injustice really are, in the sense of (a), in and for themselves, independent of their consequences. What he wants to know is "how they inwardly work in the soul." He will discuss the nature of justice in terms of its origin. He will also show that men practice justice unwillingly, out of necessity, and not because it is good. In the light of this, he will try to show that the life of injustice is better. He says that he does not agree with this view, but that he wants to make the best possible case for it, so that the refutation of it will be unshakable.

GLAUCON ON THE NATURE AND ORIGIN OF JUSTICE (358 E):
Doing an injustice is good, but suffering it is an evil. The evil

outweighs the good, so men agree to practice justice merely in order to avoid injury at one another's hands. This is why law originates.

> **COMMENT:** This is the origin of the famous Social-Contract theory in Thomas Hobbes, John Locke and Jean Jacques Rousseau—although this later development is far different from Glaucon's. The idea is also reflected in Friedrich Nietzsche's *Genealogy of Morals*, when he speaks of the morality of the weak.

Glaucon goes on to say that what all men really want is to commit injustices and to get away with them. This is the best thing of all. The worst is to suffer injustice and not to be able to do anything in retaliation. So men have hit on a compromise: justice is not a good but a lesser evil. At least we will not suffer at the hands of others.

THE MYTH OF GYGES (359 C): To show that men practice justice only because they have to, let us give to the just and to the unjust men the power to do what they want, and then let us see what they do. It will be shown that their motives are identical: self-interest. There is a myth about Gyges, a shepherd of a king. Gyges finds a mysterious ring, and puts it on. When he meets the other shepherds, he happens to turn the ring so that it is inside his hand. He instantly becomes invisible. He tests the ring repeatedly and it works. When he is sent to the court as the monthly messenger, he makes himself invisible, seduces the queen, kills the king and takes over the kingdom.

Now, let us give the just man such a ring, and the unjust man another. These men would be able to take what they wanted, to kill whom they wanted and no jail could hold them. Would the actions of the just man differ from those of the unjust man? Not at all. Having all this power, and immunity from punishment, the just man would be a fool if he remained righteous. Thus, if a man is just, it is only because he is forced to be. In their hearts, men know that injustice is far more profitable.

THE TWO KINDS OF LIFE (360 E): As a test, let us consider the life of the *perfectly* unjust man (who gets away with murder, yet is regarded as a virtuous person; this is the acme of the life of injustice) and weigh this against the life of the *per-*

fectly just man (who is virtuous, but without anyone's knowing it, so that he cannot be said to be doing it for the sake of other men's respect; his whole life long, he is the best of men, yet is considered the worst; he undergoes all sorts of torture, yet remains unshaken). Now, which man has led the happier life? Is not the unjust man (who gives the appearance of being just) given all kinds of respect in the community, and even financial credit? And since he can practice injustice without a qualm, there is no business deal he cannot make. He can become rich, make friends among the powerful, be a real threat to his enemies—in other words, he can become the world's greatest social "success."

ADEIMANTUS' CONTRIBUTION TO THIS VIEW (362 D): When parents tell their children about justice, it is not that they really advocate justice for its own sake, but rather for the sake of character and the respect of others. What they are pushing is not justice but "success." Adeimantus cites quotations from Homer and Hesiod that are usually held up as examples of justice. (In grammar school, we are often told about the worldly advantages accruing from telling truth and keeping promises.)

It is equally unscrupulous to try to sell justice on the basis of rewards in the after-life, Adeimantus says. How virtuous is virtue if it is pursued for *any* reward? When people praise justice only for its consequences, aren't they agreeing with the man who says that injustice is better because its advantages are greater? Both agree that advantage is the deciding factor, and what if it could be shown that justice has no advantages, as many laymen and poets think (364 A)? Would those who speak of its advantages continue to support it? Obviously not. Thus, the supporters of justice themselves undermine it.

> **COMMENT:** What this means is that if we pursue virtue for *any* reason (approval, reward, heaven) other than virtue itself, then we are not acting virtuously. Thus, justice must be pursued as an intrinsic good, for its own sake, not as an instrumental good—good because of . . . . This view is shared by Kant. The difference is that Adeimantus is saying justice is *always* pursued for an instrumental reason, a consideration of advantage, and so it cannot be a real virtue.

ADEIMANTUS ON RELIGION (364 C): Another way in which the concept of justice is undermined by its supporters is when they tell us that we can pray to the gods (as though the gods could be swayed against their will!), and that, if we offer sacrifices and make spectacles of ourselves, we can persuade the gods to pardon us.

What is the effect of all this on the young? If they are bright, they will see that there is no profit in being virtuous when no one knows about it. But if all I need is merely the *reputation* of being virtuous, then heaven is already mine. The mere reputation of virtue, without the practice of virtue itself, is easy enough to acquire. "Appearance tyrannizes over truth and is the lord of happiness" (365 C). Then let us devote ourselves to appearances, the young will say, and let us keep our real views to ourselves.

The young sometimes see us in courtrooms (and in politics, in advertising, in salesmanship), trying to persuade people to accept what we know is bad. Then what sort of religion can we really claim for ourselves? Someone may say that the gods are not fooled, but do we care? We ask, in return, what if there are no gods, or what if the gods have no concern for men? Then we have no cause for worry. And if there are gods, then all we know of them is what has been handed down by religious tradition, and this tells us that the gods can be swayed by prayer and sacrifices. If this is the case, and tradition is correct, then let us be unjust—"sinning and praying, praying and sinning" (366A).

As intelligent men, therefore, ought we not to laugh when we hear justice being praised—when it is foolish to do anything other than injustice? The only one who finds fault with injustice is the man who lacks the power to be unjust himself. The proof is that as soon as a just man gets the power, he is as unjust as anyone else.

THE PSYCHOLOGICAL BASIS IS WHAT WE SEEK: Of all the poets and writers, no one has ever praised justice for itself, but only for the benefits that flow from it. Nobody has ever praised justice on the basis of the way it actually works in the soul of man, and shown that its effect is psychologically good, while the effect of injustice is psychologically bad. Adeimantus says he speaks so strongly about this because he wants to be convinced that justice is psychologically beneficial, and injustice psychologically harmful to its practitioners.

SOCRATES' REPLY (368 A):   What is demanded, then, is an answer to a two-fold problem: first, the nature of justice and injustice; second, their relative advantages. Socrates, pointing to his own inabilities, decides to magnify the problem, so that he can see its "letters," its details, more clearly. *He assumes that he can equate virtue in the individual with virtue in the state. The state is nothing more than a blown-up version of the individual.* Since the state is large, the justice in it will be more easily discernible. Let us see how a state arises, and how justice appears in it.

THE STATE ARISES: A state arises in order to serve human needs: men band together to help themselves live better and thus arises an interchange of food, shelter and clothing—each man supplying the wants of another. If a man lives with four others, he will not produce food only for himself, and spend the rest of the time building his house and making his clothes. It is more natural for one man to prepare food for all, while another makes clothes for all, etc.

> **COMMENT:**   Even in this rudimentary state, there is already a division of labor. We see here the germ of an idea that will be of great importance later. Socrates will eventually use the principle of the division of labor in his condemnation of democracy. Where every man does everything (in Athens, carpenters could be judges for a day), no man does anything well. As shoemakers are trained for their work, so should rulers be trained for theirs—and each should do what he is trained for, each according to his "nature." Work is done better when the workman practices only his skill and no other.

THE STATE GROWS: With this growth, there is a corresponding differentiation of needs. The farmer no longer makes his own plow; now there is a skilled artisan making agricultural implements. The same goes for the other skills: each requires the services of another. Now, there are tradesmen, merchants, shippers, jobbers, credit houses, etc. Thus, the state grows and requires more services. And these, in turn, enlarge the state.

THE STATE IS MATURE: Where, in all this, does justice come in? Probably in men's dealings with one another. As to the state itself, now that it has supplied the bare necessities, men will want the conveniences of life. This leads ultimately to demands for luxury. Soon we have artists, actors, poets, dancers, courtesans. Now we want barbers and tutors, confectioners and cooks—and with these latter two we want, of course, physicians.

This means that the original, healthy state is no longer self-sufficient. It must enlarge its borders, and will need its neighbor's land for pasture and tillage. Since the neighbors want this land, this leads to war. Thus, war is derived from economic causes. (Compare with Marx.) For war, we need professional soldiers, not a rag-tag citizen army (such as is the norm in democratic Athens). These soldiers will have to be trained for their work.

THE TRAINING OF SOLDIERS: We must select those who will have fighting spirit. But even here, we need men who will have the intelligence to distinguish friends from enemies—like dogs who are gentle with their masters and angry with strangers. The dog, Socrates says, is a kind of philosopher! He distinguishes friend from enemy on the basis of evidence: his knowing or not knowing the person approaching (376 B). In the same way, the soldier must have not only spirit but knowledge as well. How are men to be trained for this? (In the answer to this question we will see the nature of justice and injustice in states.) Let us give them gymnastic training for the body, and music (the composite term for literature) for their souls. (Observe how deftly Socrates has made the transition from description of a real state to description of an ideal state.)

What sort of literature? We begin by telling children fairy-tales, usually. Should we? This is an important decision to make, for it is at this stage that character is formed in children. We cannot allow them to hear just any kind of story. We must therefore establish some sort of control, a censorship of what our children are to hear. At this stage, forming the mind is more important than forming the body.

SOCRATES' CRITICISM OF TRADITIONAL LITERATURE: Can we have Homer and Hesiod? No, for although they are great poets, they portray the gods as doing terrible things: Cronus castrating his father, Uranus; Hephaestus tying up his mother, Hera; Hera being beaten by Zeus; the gods generally fighting amongst themselves. Are these proper tales for the ears of children? Young children cannot always tell the difference between truth and allegory; all this might be real to them.

> COMMENT: Socrates is quite "modern" about all this. Consider the effects of comic books and TV. A prominent psychologist, Frederic Wertheim, maintains that when children see violence on TV, they accept it as reality. He contends that the level of violence in the actual crimes committed has risen drastically because of this, that there is an increasing amount of sadism in even ordinary stick-ups. Moreover, Socrates' point is challenging for another reason: the works of Homer and Hesiod occupied an educational function similar to that occupied by the Bible in the centuries previous to our own. Following the examples of Socrates, ought we to ban stories about the polygamy of Abraham and Jacob, the drunkenness of Noah, etc.? Ought we to ban the Sermon on the Mount as tending to weaken the fighting spirit? We might, at first, want to censor comic books, but if it means that we can also censor Homer, *Lady Chatterley's Lover*, or *Das Kapital*, do we then want to censor them? What Socrates feels he is advocating, then, is an enlightened application of morality to education.

WHAT THE POETS OUGHT TO SHOW: The poets ought rather to show that the gods never quarrel. The gods must always be portrayed as they are: truly good, not malicious, the creators only of good, not of evil. Homer talks about Zeus sending both good and evil to man. God can send punishment to wrongdoers to correct them—which is a good thing, but God must not be shown as sending evil indiscriminately. Nor can we allow our poets to show the gods telling lies, or transforming themselves, or changing their appearance. What is good and perfect does not change. If God, who is good and perfect, were to change, it could only be for the worse, since the perfect cannot be better.

These stories of Homer and Hesiod are lies of the worst sort, and there is no excuse for them. God does not lie, or deceive, or change. Although we may admire Homer's skill, we must not accept his lies about God.

> COMMENT: What Socrates has done is to ban the entire pantheon as it is understood in his time. To get the full im-

pact of this, we need only ask ourselves how far we would
be willing to go in giving up our biblical personages and
incidents for the sake of proper education.

THE REPUBLIC, BOOK III

This book gives the appearance of being a rather abstract discussion, full of literary references and talk about aesthetic
styles. But these problems all relate to our discussion of the
state in a direct way. To begin with, we must see to it that the
poets praise the life hereafter, rather than condemn it. We cannot have our soldiers being afraid of death. The famous statement of Homer's, that he would rather be a slave among the
living than rule as king of the dead, is not to be accepted in our
state.

> **COMMENT:** For the Greeks, the world below was not
> one of punishment and reward, but rather a gray, dusty
> place in which the disembodied souls hovered "like
> smoke." No hell was needed, since there was punishment
> enough in being deprived of earthly life; and no heaven
> was needed, since no reward could possibly make up for
> the deprivation of life. In Book X, though, Plato intro-
> duces the concept of reward and punishment in the after-
> life.

We cannot have our soldiers fearing death as the worst evil;
they must fear defeat and enslavement more than death (387
B). Since we do not want the after-life to be feared, we must
not have our soldiers grieving at the death of a comrade or
kinsman. So we must not have scenes such as the one in
Homer, where Achilles grieves at the death of Patroclus, and
puts handfuls of ashes on his head. This and many other such
scenes in Homer must be rejected, for the young are
undoubtedly impressed by them and might be tempted to act in
the same way when the occasion arises.

POETIC LIES: The only justification for lying is when we do
so for therapeutic reasons. But as medicine is dispensed properly only by physicians, so the privilege of dispensing a lie
should rest only with the rulers, who, if they must lie, will do
so only for the public good. For a citizen to lie to the rulers
would be like a patient lying to his own physician. This is why
we must not permit lying by our subjects, cobblers or poets.

Lying should be reserved only for the rulers. (Socrates has already advocated censorship, now he advocates the right of rulers to dispense propaganda.)

The poets show the gods being intemperate and giving way to lust. We can have none of this. Nor are we going to let them sing the praises of money and gifts, and portray our heroes as being bought for money.

COMMENT: Socrates cites example after example from Homer. Since manuscripts were rare and expensive, most Greeks learned their Homer by hearing the verses recited. It was commonplace, therefore, for most any Greek to develop a memory that would be considered prodigious today. Socrates is not reading from a book. He knows these lines by heart, and many more, and so does Adeimantus. He is like a man who knows his Bible, throwing out one cherished scene after another. His purpose here is not simply to attack the tenets of religion but to decide what we must give up for the sake of a proper education. Oughtn't we, for example, to censor the scene in which Abraham, simply because God has commanded him to do so, is ready to cut the throat of his son, Isaac?

Nor can we have scenes of bestiality, such as that in which Achilles dishonors the body of the fallen Hector by dragging it in the dust, letting the head batter along the ground; nor the scene in which he slaughters the captive Trojans at the funeral pyre of Patroclus. If the gods and heroes do such things, may we not expect the young to emulate them and to defend their actions by these examples (391 E)?

Similar lies are perpetrated by poets when they tell us that wicked men are happy and good men are miserable, or that injustice is profitable when undetected, and justice is not. But fuller criticism of this will have to wait until we return to our original question: how does justice work in the soul?

POETIC STYLE: In the meantime, there is a discussion of the styles of poetic writing. We must keep in mind, in all this, the emphasis which Socrates gives to the psychological effect of the various art forms. If we enjoy an art form that is totally unreal, must not our sense of reality become distorted? Ought we not, therefore, to allow only those art forms that give us our greatest contact with reality, those that put no screen between ourselves and the world?

Now, poetry uses the art of imitation, as when the poet speaks in the persons of his characters rather than narrating the story in his own words (392 D). Socrates says that we ought to have only straight exposition, not dramatic representation. If a writer wants to say that the world is a, b, and c, then let him say so in his own person, *presenting* the words as his own, rather than putting them in the mouth of his characters, so that the ideas are *represented* rather than presented.

> **COMMENT:** One of the difficulties in reading a work that is in dialogue form is the problem of determining which character it is that represents the view of the author. Remember that Plato had stated, in one of his letters, that the *Dialogues* do not represent his own philosophy! Another point: in Plato's condemnation of dramatic representation, in favor of direct presentation, must not the *Republic* itself be condemned as a work of dramatic representation? Certainly, Plato must have realized this. What is the answer to this enigma? Did Plato have some special purpose that is far from obvious? Could it be that the *Republic* is really a kind of satire on itself, and on all social planning?

His condemnation of imitation will have important implications later on, when the theory of the forms of reality is discussed. The point which Socrates is making here is that art involves a kind of imitation, and imitation is not reality. (This is not a merely abstract point. Is there not a danger that in seeing lots of murders on TV, murder itself may become as acceptable as the representation of it? Presumably, according to Plato's thinking, our impressionable youngsters might commit murder as easily as they watch it committed—since they do most of their living in this unreal TV world.)

Imitation can have bad effects. Shouldn't it be prohibited? Our imitations become part of our nature (395 D). We have heroes whose mannerisms become part of us. Someone innocently crosses us, let us say; we react with the calm ruthlessness of a James Bond. How, then, do we weigh the psychological harm of all this violence—whether from the Bible, Shakespeare, or "007"—against the benefit of a free choice in an open society?

How far are we prepared to go for the sake of a system of education that could give us perfection? What sacrifices are we prepared to make?

OUGHT OUR GUARDIANS TO BE IMITATORS? (394 E):

Doesn't a politician devote a lot of attention to his "image"? An actor can play many parts. But what happens when politicians become actors? The state suffers. The guardians of the state ought to have as their primary concern the maintenance of freedom, not the projection of an "image." The only characteristics they ought to imitate are courage, temperance, piety, freedom, and the like. If the ruler spends much time on his "image" there is less of a sense of reality that he devotes to his duties.

When these false poets and actors come to our state, let us therefore show them great respect but tell them that our state will not allow them to perform (398 A). For the health of our souls we need a different kind of poet and story-teller.

ART'S PSYCHOLOGICAL EFFECT JUSTIFIES OUR CONTROL OF IT:

Socrates' basic idea in all this is that different art forms have variously powerful effects on the soul. Certain kinds of music are to be banned as being too sensual, luxurious, or effeminate. We ought to have marches during wartime, hymns and "mood-music" during peace. On the grounds of taste, we might condemn this sort of choice in a free society. But the point, once more, is this: what sacrifices are we prepared to make for perfection?

> **COMMENT:** It is only in the relative security of a democracy that a people can refuse to allow their government to institute censorship. Internally weaker forms of government, e.g., Soviet Russia and Nazi Germany, being aware of the capacity of the arts to influence men's character, morality and political beliefs, have responded by severely censoring all art works. It seems to be a truism that a society's internal cohesiveness is inversely proportional to the degree of its censorship: the weaker the society, the stronger the censorship. How strong is the Republic in that case?

The state is being purged of its unnecessary luxuries, Socrates says (399 E). Our music must have a proper harmony and rhythm: one based upon simplicity. The same is to be done to the other arts, such as painting and sculpture. We cannot have these show moral depravity, lest it corrupt our souls (401 C). (Socrates would not think, for example, that when we see depravity in a play by Tennessee Williams, we are purged of similar depravity in ourselves.)

HARMONY IN THE SOUL: What are the various forms of courage, temperance, and so on? We must learn to recognize them in their varied combinations. Having this kind of knowledge is what we mean by having music in one's soul—having a soul that is perfectly harmonized in its many aspects. Socrates is using the language of lovers (403 A), but what he is really talking about is the integration of the various faculties so as to form a well-harmonized soul. This is "mental health" in its truest sense. The neurotic person emphasizes one aspect so that it takes over his life. But in the healthy person, each function has its proper expression. Thus, there is in the individual psyche the principle of division of labor, each aspect doing its part. If a man spends all his time proving his courage, his courage is to be doubted. It is equally sick of the psyche as it is of the state, if one faculty, or virtue, or class take on an overriding importance at the expense of the whole. Socrates takes this discussion on to the level of gymnastic training, but the goal is the same (403 D).

> **COMMENT:** On the temple of Apollo, at Delphi, there were two inscriptions which Socrates took for his own mottoes, although he interpreted them in a special way. The inscriptions were: (a) "Know thyself," and (b) "Nothing in excess." For the devotees of Apollo, these inscriptions had a religious significance. They meant, in effect: (a_1) "Know who you are: a mere mortal in the presence of the gods," and (b_1) "See to it that you do not overstep your mortal limitations by trying to be like god, for this is hubris." For Socrates, however, these mottoes take on a psychological meaning: (a_2) "All virtue is knowledge. The virtues of a man can be based only on his knowledge of himself," and (b_2) "Excess destroys the soul's harmony." It is moderation that we are to follow, for psychological rather than religious reasons.

THE CARE OF THE SOUL: This is the most important concern a man can have. (Socrates often speaks of himself as a physician and uses analogies from medicine.) Physicians cure bodily diseases, judges cure some diseases of disharmonized souls. (Incidentally, it is Socrates who is the first to consider the psychological origin of the criminal act.) The existence of physicians and judges indicates the sickness of a society. It is only in societies with a great deal of leisure that we find these physical and social ills (406 D), ills that indicate luxury and self-indulgence. A society ought rather to be like a lean and hard workman, too busy to be sick; and if he is sick, desirous of a quick and simple cure. He and society should have no time for extended pampering.

THE TRAINING OF GUARDIANS: Their training involves music (poetry) for the soul and gymnastics for the body. Each of these disciplines can be harmful if taken by itself. At the beginning, the mind seems sharper, the body toned up. But if either discipline is carried further, a man can become too sensitive or effeminate in soul, or else too stupid and brutalized in body. Our guardians will combine these disciplines, thereby avoiding the dangers inherent in each when taken in isolation.

The ones we train for public service must be under constant observation, and pass all kinds of trials. They must be tested with enticements, temptations and terrors, to see how they will stand up. From among these men we will choose our leaders. Let us call these leaders our "guardians," and the others, whom we were calling "guardians" until now, let us call them "auxiliaries." The latter will carry out the decisions of the guardians.

THE NOBLE LIE (414 C):   To accomplish this division into classes (the guardians, the auxiliaries, and the populace), we shall have to resort to a lie. Socrates is quite embarrassed at this. He would not propose this if he did not think it necessary. How else will the populace accept this division into classes, with themselves in the lowest? Let us tell them that they were all born from the earth, who is their real mother. (Adeimantus agrees that this is a shameful lie. What would it do to children's love for their parents?) There is worse to come, Socrates says. We shall say that the rulers are superior because when they were in earth there was gold mixed into them. The auxiliaries will be told that they have silver in them, the populace that they have iron and brass. It is true that gold parents might have mere silver sons, but we will find this out while we are observing and testing them. (Socrates says nothing of brass parents producing gold offspring.)

The rulers must be careful to guard the purity of the race. We must not let the men of brass and iron rule the state, for if they do, they will destroy it.

> **COMMENT:** This is, of course, a condemnation of democracy. Many men today *respect* democracy; Plato doesn't, let us remember, for the Athenian experiment with democracy was the first of its kind and he saw it collapse in defeat, a victim, he felt, of the men of brass and iron. And it was the Athenian democracy, remember, that had executed Socrates. This form of the caste system, however, is difficult to understand in the light of what Socrates says later on: talented children are selected for training regardless of who their parents were.

Is there any chance, Socrates asks, of getting the populace to sit still for this lie? Adeimantus thinks not, certainly not in this generation anyway.

SAFEGUARDS: What safeguards can we impose to make sure that the rulers never become tyrants? Adeimantus says that education is not enough, since when they become tyrants they have already been educated. Socrates has greater faith in the deterrent influence of education, but he suggests that their way of life, also, should be arranged in such a way as to discourage the growth of the ills we usually see in states. As the greatest influence for corruption of government officers is ownership of property this ownership must be forbidden. They must have no property, whether money, land, houses or anything else, and must live on a minimal wage, sleep in barracks and eat in a common mess hall.

> **COMMENT:** What rulers in the real world would stand for this? But that is the point, precisely. This picture shows us how far from the ideal we really are. This, impossible as it is, is what people would have to do to make a state perfect. All of the *Republic* is hyperbole in this same sense. It is like saying, "The only way there will ever be peace is to cut everybody's arms off." In the same tone, Plato is saying, "The only way there will ever be

honest government is if the rulers own nothing but the clothes they stand in."

THE REPUBLIC, BOOK IV

There are three main points in this book: (1) a new definition of happiness: the harmonious integration of all elements; (2) the correlation of the state with the individual soul, so that whatever applies to the one will be found to apply to the other; (3) a discussion of the way in which the virtues act in the state and in the soul.

Plato's treatment of the first two points is certainly novel and unique. The points, however, are not novel at all, but are the spun-out implications of an idea that was basic to the Greek way of life (although the idea was not often made explicit).

IDENTITY OF ETHICS AND POLITICS: The basic idea referred to is the view that ethics and politics are the same, or at least co-terminous (overlapping in essential features). There was no distinction between private life and public life, as there is today. There was no such concept as the "invasion of privacy," perhaps because no Athenian felt that he had a private life that was to be kept distinct from his public life. Today, we might put our personal relationships ahead of our civic responsibilities, our private loyalties ahead of our public loyalties. In the *Greek* city-state no man would do this. (It is this which can explain to those of us who feel alienated from our society, because we regard it as being something "other" than ourselves, why it is that Socrates refuses to escape from prison when he is offered the chance. And it seems clear that no man who accepts the distinction between his private and public life would be able to live in the Republic.)

For the Greek, therefore, the *polis* is part of oneself. In the Funeral Oration given by Pericles (at the services for the warriors fallen in the first year of the Peloponnesian War, 431 B.C.), he describes the Athenian way of life, and shows how an Athenian's existence is thoroughly bound up with that of the state. In the twentieth century, a man might take no part in public life and regard himself as being happy; certainly, he would not necessarily think of his life as being a failure because of it. For the Athenians, however, a man who takes no part in public affairs is not merely unambitious, Pericles says; "such a man is useless."

PLATO ON THE IDENTITY OF ETHICS AND POLITICS: The rules of the private and public worlds, the principles of ethics and politics, are part of one another, in the Greek view. If ethics and politics are the same, then it follows that the concept of virtue must be the same for both. And what distorts and corrupts an individual would have the same affect on the state. What is new in Plato's treatment of the idea is that:

(1) He is making the identity of state and soul explicit by finding similarities in their structure. The state is merely the soul magnified, "writ large."

(2) He regards the two sciences relative to them as being reducible to one another: that is, personal psychology and political theory are one and the same in basis.

(3) He makes explicit the implications of this state/soul identity. If certain things are true about the structure of men's souls then certain other things will have to be true about the structure of the state.

(4) The best state is the one that is structured in accordance with the pattern of the soul's structure. Such a state conforms to "human nature."

THE QUESTION OF HAPPINESS: Adeimantus begins the discussion by wondering whether the people that would live in the Republic would be happy at all. After they have pared down their way of life to the bare essentials, they must be utterly miserable. They have nothing in the way of comforts; their life is like that of the Spartans.

Socrates adds to his Spartan view of the guardian's life by pointing out that they will get no pay for their services, and so will have no money to spend on luxuries and mistresses. Yet they may be the happiest of men, Socrates says. What we are aiming for is the happiness of the state as a whole, not the happiness of one class, and it is to derive its happiness from the fact that it *is* a whole. We shall see that it is in a state that is organized for the good of the whole that we shall find justice—and with it, happiness.

Accordingly, if we pity the guardians because they lack luxuries, we are missing the point. A life of sensuality and opulence would make them no longer guardians, but something as bizarre as shepherds wearing crowns. The crowns would do violence to their reality; the shepherds could no longer be happy as shepherds. It is much worse for the state when the guardians depart from reality, and men in constant revelry are not men who are citizens in a harmonious society. Happiness is measured not in terms of individuals but rather in terms of the wholeness of the state.

SPECIFIC POINTS ABOUT THE STATE (421 D):   (1) Wealth and poverty tend to corrupt an artisan. The rulers must guard against these extremes in the state as a whole. It is to be neither too rich nor too poor.

(2) War: most Greek city-states do not have standing armies. It is the citizens who fight. Since these spend most of their time at earning their livelihood, they cannot devote much time to military training and therefore will not make efficient soldiers. The Republic, however, has an army that is trained, so it will always have the advantage over any untrained army, even if the latter is bigger. Also, the Republic can combine with allies in time of war. It will attract allies because it has better fighters, and because its enemies are richer, there will be more in the way of spoils when it wins. "Who would choose to fight against lean wiry dogs, rather than *with* the dogs against fat and tender sheep?" Another advantage the Republic has is this: it is one state, completely unified, whereas other states are composed of classes that are hostile to one another: the rich and the poor. The Republic can combine with either class against the other, fighting from within. (Athens and Sparta each pursued such tactics in the Peloponnesian War.)

(3) Size of the state: its territory is to be only so large as is consistent with unity and self-sufficiency.

(4) Social mobility: inferior offspring of guardians are to be down-graded; no man is to be made a guardian simply because his father was one. And superior offspring of the populace are to be elevated, to be taken into the ranks of trainees, as potential guardians. Each man is to be put to the use for which nature has best prepared him.

(5) Specialization: consider Huxley's *Brave New World*, a novel about a state in which men are bred for certain levels of intelligence. There is then no chance of a brilliant individual having to run an elevator because he happened to be born into a socially or economically deprived class. The advantage of such eugenic planning, therefore, is that it eliminates a possible waste to be found in free societies. In Plato's state, likewise, each man is to do the work for which he is best suited (though what he is best suited for will not be eugenically planned by the government). And he is to do *only* that. We shall not have, as we do in democratic states, men being both carpenters and judges. Such a system can lead only to bad carpentry and bad law. Each man should be one man, not many men. If each man is one, not many, then the state will be one, not many (423 D).

THE ROLE OF EDUCATION: All of the foregoing is part of one great principle—education, *paideia*. If our citizens are raised as sensible men, they will easily see the wisdom of all this. Good education leads to good government, and good government leads, in turn, to good education. In this way, the breed of men is improved. (This is another instance of the identity of ethics and politics, for the function of the state is to make men good.)

As to the form of education, we must keep to the traditional modes in music (poetry) and gymnastics, and shun novelties. When the forms of music (or any of the basic art-forms) change, then the fundamental laws change with them. (Here, again, we have Plato's emphasis on the psychological effect of art.) License in art breeds license in customs, then license in the keeping of contracts, then license in laws, then a recklessness ending in chaos and the overthrow of all rights. But a sense of order in the way we let our youngsters play will ultimately contribute to a sense of order in society. The way in which education begins in a man will determine his future life, so we should ingrain this sense of order. Without it, we will have not a society but a hodge-podge.

What we usually find is a kind of patchwork—patching here, leaking there. Such a society is like an invalid—doctoring itself here, getting sick there; and like a hypochondriac, or a professional alcoholic, it will never get on its feet, will never learn to control itself or avoid self-indulgence. And, like a hypochondriac or an alcoholic, such a society will fly into a rage when anyone tells it the truth about itself. (Socrates can draw this analogy because he talks about states as though they were individual souls.) In such states, the men who cater to the whims of the hypochondriac state will be called great statesmen (the way such patients call quacks great doctors), and these "great statesmen" may even come to believe this about themselves. They will think that they can cure these gigantic social ills by patchwork medicine, a treatment that actually only prolongs and promotes the ills.

JUSTICE: Where is justice in our Republic? Let us search for it. The search will be the same for the state as for the individual soul. Just as it was shown that happiness in the state was not to be confined to one class so happiness in the individual is not to be confined to one function, like the gratification of the senses alone. The good state has the same four virtues of the good individual: it is wise and courageous and temperate and just.

WISDOM IN THE STATE (428 B): Wisdom is a kind of knowledge. But it is not like a knowledge of carpentry nor like any knowledge of a particular craft. (Nor should we, I think, in the twentieth century, treat social wisdom as a kind of technology or social work.) The kind of knowledge we need is a knowledge of the way in which the *entire* state is to be organized and run. And this wisdom is the province of the guardians, the smallest class. When these are wise, the whole state can be said to be wise.

COURAGE IN THE STATE (429 A): Courage, too, is a kind of knowledge. In the individual, it is the ability to distinguish true from false dangers, a knowledge of when to go forward, despite dangers, and when to hold back. In the state, we might say that such knowledge tells us what goals to pursue. This courage is the province of the auxiliaries (who are not only the military but also the executives and civil service). It is these men who make the state as a whole either a brave or cowardly, judicious or recklessly foolish one.

TEMPERANCE IN THE STATE (430 E): In the individual, temperance is the control of desires, self-mastery, an obedience to the best impulses in oneself, not the worst—that is, an obedience to reason. It functions in the same way in the state, making the state as a whole either sober or self-destructive. Actually, the virtue of temperance in the state is not something distinct from the other virtues, or we would have the strange sight of a state that could be wise and yet intemperate.

Temperance is a virtue that is to be found in the rulers as well as in the subjects (431 A). But since the guardians and auxiliaries already have their distinctive virtues—wisdom and courage—then there remains for the populace only the empty function of obedience. It is an empty function in the way that being a patient is an empty function in the practice of medicine. Yet, if the guardians alone can exercise wisdom, and if the auxiliaries alone can make executive and military decisions, then what can we leave for the populace to *do*? The audience to whom the *Republic* was addressed were Greeks all of whom were accustomed to playing an active role in public life, for even the carpenters were judges and members of the Assembly. What Plato is asking them to do, if it can be considered a "doing" at all, is to function in a way that is totally strange to an Athenian. Many of us will recall that in singing class, in elementary or junior-high school, we were divided into sopranos, altos, tenors, baritones—and "listeners," a seemingly active title for those who could not participate because they had no ear. This temperance, then, this obedience, is such a "doing:" a totally passive role of non-participation.

JUSTICE IN THE STATE (432 D):   This, too, is not a virtue of any one class, but is rather a characteristic of the state as a whole. It has to do with a situation in which each man does his proper work, as each part of the soul does its proper work. We do not expect our senses to do our reasoning, as we do not expect our desires to function in place of our eyes and ears. When each does the work it is fitted to do, we have a psychologically healthy individual.

In the same way, we must not expect warriors to do the work of rulers, nor rulers to do the work of warriors. Nor are tradesmen fit to do the work of either of these classes; if they try to they can ruin the state. In the same way, to complete the analogy, no part of the soul ought to do the work of another. This principle of justice is the same for states as for individuals (434 D).

STATE AND SOUL: If what Socrates says is true, that justice is the same for states as for individuals, it ought to be possible to find a similarity of structure between states and individual souls, and, most important of all, to find that the same virtues apply to both! The individual has three parts to his soul, as does the state (435 C):

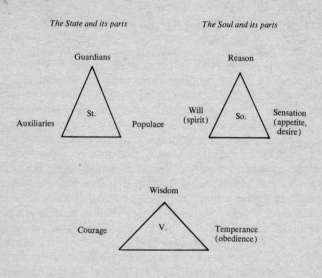

The State and its parts   *The Soul and its parts*

Guardians   Reason

Auxiliaries   St.   Populace   Will (spirit)   So.   Sensation (appetite, desire)

Wisdom

Courage   V.   Temperance (obedience)

Virtues of the State and of the Soul

Wisdom is the virtue of guardians in our state, as it is the virtue relating to the proper use of reason in the soul (441 C). Courage is the virtue of auxiliaries in the state as it is the virtue relating to the proper exercise of the will in the soul (441 D). Temperance is the virtue reserved for the populace as it is the virtue pertaining to the proper use of the senses in the soul. Justice is the same for the state as for the individual soul: each part doing its proper work to achieve a harmonious whole (441 D). (This shows us, also, that our ideal Republic, where the qualification for rulers is wisdom, nothing else, is closest in structure to "human nature," the structure of the individual soul. Any state in which rulers occupy their position by any other means, i.e., not wisdom, but wealth, inherited title or the approval of the people, is a distortion of what a state *should* be, it is a departure from "human nature.")

THE RULE OF REASON: Further, it is clear that as reason ought to rule in the soul, so the wisdom of the guardians *ought* to rule in a state (441 E). "They are the shepherds, and the auxiliaries are the dogs who heed their voice" (440 C), and presumably help to keep the sheep together. The section from 436 A to 441 C is concerned with distinguishing the parts of the soul. In a disordered soul, there would be conflict between these parts. Sometimes, a certain part of the soul will unite with another against the third, as do factions in a state (440 B). But in a well-ordered state, as in the harmonious soul, the whole is ruled by the highest principle: reason, the guardians. And as the appetites ought to obey reason in the soul, so they ought to obey it in the state. They will be brought into harmony by our system of training: music and gymnastics. A man trained in this way will find justice a part of his nature.

THRASYMACHUS AND GLAUCON ARE NOW ANSWERED: This, then, is Socrates' answer to Thrasymachus and Glaucon. They had said that it would be natural for a man to steal and kill if he could get away with it. Since this is *natural*, then all law is artificial, a matter of human *convention* and construction (which explains the differences between one culture and another). But Socrates has now shown that it is more natural for a man to be just rather than unjust if his soul is healthy and each part is doing its proper work (443 D). Such a man would find it "unnatural" to steal. He is his own master, he gives law to himself and he obeys it—and so he is at peace with himself. Justice in the soul is therefore a matter of psychological balance and perfection, as injustice is imbalance and disorder. To call imbalance natural, as Thrasymachus and Glaucon did, is like calling disease natural. True, there *are* diseased human beings, but the truly natural condition is health.

Which is more profitable, justice or injustice? The question is now ridiculous. It is like asking, "which is more profitable, health or illness."

THE REPUBLIC, BOOK V

This book occupies an intermediate position, between pure theory and pinpoint detail. It is still wrapped up in precise "How-to-Run-a-State" instructions on matters we saw raised in Book IV. And yet, the present book is concerned with such seemingly abstract matters as the unity of a state and the meaning of wisdom. Many of the expectations built up in Book IV remain unsatisfied here, however. Why doesn't Plato continue the psychological discussion? Why doesn't he define just what he means by wisdom? The present book only suggests what wisdom is, and only in the last few pages. Why, then, has Plato written Book V so unevenly?

The answer is that he must have precisely such a book to allow us to make the transition from descriptive detail to abstract theory. The definition of wisdom, the nature of knowledge and reality—all these theoretical problems will be given their due later on. He must first prepare us for this by showing how the matter-of-fact details *demand* a theoretical discussion. He handles such a transition in a masterful way: the bubbling details are cooled by breaths of theory; the icy abstractions are warmed by showing us their day-to-day applications.

Socrates is concerned, here, with a lengthy description of the guardians' family life. This makes a proper sequel to Book IV, which described their education. Socrates suggests, however, that he is not *merely* concerned with matters of detail, even though he is forced to spend so much time on them. A point we must keep in mind is a statement made by Socrates: all this description displays an ideal, for the sole purpose of showing us how far from the ideal we actually are.

THE IDEAL: The question, therefore, of whether such a state can ever come into existence is not a question at all. He is not drawing us a blueprint from which we might build an actual state. All he is doing is holding a mirror up to nature (human nature). That is why he can permit himself to spend so much time on a topic that must have seemed to the Greeks to be little more than science-fiction: the question of the equality of women. It is because this work is *not* intended as a blueprint for an actual state that such a topic *can* find a place here. In the Greek world, such an idea was not even a topic for controversy—it was simply beyond consideration altogether. Besides the traditional limits to the equality of women, there was one practical limitation: they just never got the education given to men. Plato is therefore concerned to have his readers see, in a very direct way, what a difference there is between the ideal and the actual.

Undoubtedly, the Athenians were as proud of their democracy as we are of our republic. Indeed, we can imagine that they must have been even prouder, since it was they who thought up the idea of freedom. What Plato is doing, therefore, is showing them how far their achievement is from perfection, how far they would have to go before they could claim real pride in their creation: men can claim pride only in a government that conforms to the highest in man's nature, and such a government, he tells us, can never come into existence!

THE DISCUSSION: Socrates begins by suggesting that as there are four virtues, so there must be four evils. (Are there actual states corresponding to these evils in men's souls?) Adeimantus interrupts and asks for clarification of a point made earlier about the guardians having women and children in common. He wants to know about the family life of the guardians. One of the safeguards against the possible corruption of the guardians was the suggestion that they own no property. (When a politician owns a piece of property near the site of a proposed housing project, might it not affect his decision as to *where* that project is to be erected?) Another safeguard against corruption is the idea that the guardians are not to have families in our sense. (When a politician has children, could he be enough of a man of iron principle not to favor them with certain advantages?) The guardians are therefore to have wives and children in common.

WOMEN SHOULD BE GUARDIANS: A female dog is as good at watching a flock as is a male dog. A mare can pull a wagon as well as a stallion can. Since we make no sexual distinction in the tasks we assign to animals, why should we make a sexual distinction in the abilities of humans? Let us therefore give women the same duties in our state as we give men, and let them therefore have the same education. Ought women to be taught music and gymnastics, together with military arts? Shall we let them go naked on the wrestling ground, as men do? This might seem absurd at the start, especially to see old women exercising with old men, but we can get used to it.

OBJECTIONS: Our opponents might remind us that we had said that one ought to do the work suited to one's nature (453 C). Different natures ought to do different work, we had said. But let us first consider what we mean by "different and same natures." By the word "different," we refer only to differences that are significant to the tasks at hand. Just because bald men happen to be carpenters, it does not follow that hairy men cannot be carpenters. Just because men differ from women in regard to who begets and who bears children, it does not follow that this difference ought to be the basis of all differentiation. Nor should this sexual difference be reflected in the education that is given to them.

What difference is there between men and women that makes a difference in political life? (455 A.) There is no special political faculty possessed by one sex. The gifts of nature are to be found in both sexes, except that women are *generally* inferior in strength. Undoubtedly there is a particular woman (Miss K) that is superior to a particular man (Mr. L). Each person is to be considered on the basis of his or her merits. The education that makes a man a good guardian will make a woman a good guardian, if their original capacities are the same. Let them share in the toils of war, and so on (475 A), and in all other work, except that the weaker are to be given lighter tasks.

WIVES AND CHILDREN IN COMMON: Now that we have the foregoing question settled, there is an even more controversial point to consider: the guardians are to have wives and children in common, so that no parent knows his own child (475 D). Holding aside the question as to whether this is possible, let us consider the advantages.

Rulers must know how to submit and obey, in addition to knowing how to rule. The rulers will submit to having no private property, and all will live together in a community, sleeping in barracks and eating in mess halls. In this way, men and women who are rulers will come into daily contact. How are we to pair them off? Animals are mated with a view to the qualities of the offspring. For the same reason, rulers ought to submit to selected pairing by means of marriages directed by the other rulers. (Marriage by committee!)

And as the rulers must resort to therapeutic lies when dealing with society, so there must be something similar here: for the good of the state, we must keep it a secret whose child is whose. We must separate the offspring of superior parents from those of inferior parentage. All this will be kept secret. No mother will recognize her own child.

COMMENT: Needless to say, this ruthless program of eugenic control will effect only the rulers, since they alone are in the position to make the decisions which could be influenced by family connections. The populace, presumably, will have families as well as property in the conventional sense.

Some commentators believe that Plato is advocating a totalitarian state with communistic features. To these charges it may be replied: First, Plato is not *advocating* anything, as we saw. He is not talking about a state that could be, or should be, created. He is describing an idea in order to show us how imperfect we are. (Is it not true that property and family ties *do* in fact account for much of the corruption of public servants?) Second, Plato's state is not totalitarian since the controls he describes do not touch the majority of the population—only the rulers, who are to make the greatest sacrifices. In a totalitarian state, it is the populace that makes the sacrifices. Not so, in this case. (Where is the *Politburo* that would stand for Plato's demands on them?) Third, when classic communism speaks of the abolition of private property, it replaces this with government ownership and control of the means of production. This is possible only in a highly developed industrial society. No such situation is possible in the Greek context, obviously. Moreover, it is not property, as such, that is abolished in Plato's state, but only the property of the guardians.

THE MATING OF THE GUARDIANS: The prime of life for child bearing is, in a woman, the period from twenty years to forty. For a man it is the period from twenty-five to fifty-five. These are the best years of physical and intellectual vigor, and it is within these age limits that we shall pair off our guardians. Beyond these age limits we shall let them form any liaison they care to—except for those that would be incestuous—always with the understanding that we cannot allow a foetus of such a union to be born. How will we know which marriage is incestuous? Let every man consider *all* children born between the seventh and tenth months after his marriage to be *his* children, and let these children call one another "brothers" and "sisters" (regardless of who their actual parents were). These will be forbidden to marry their "parents."

However, someone can reply to this defense as follows: First, even if we grant that Plato isn't advocating that we set up such a state we can still ask about the meaning of his theory and what kind of a state we would have if we actually tried to set it up.

Secondly, though some of the controls will be inflicted only upon the guardians, there are many controls that will be applied to the entire population. (And in Plato's last work, the Laws, he greatly increases the number of controls and the severity of the punishment violators will receive.) In addition, isn't Plato's theory fundamentally totalitarian because it says that no man has inviolable, individual rights? The government may do anything to anyone as long as it says it is acting in the "public interest," and the victim of such an action cannot go to court to protect his rights. (Remember that Plato even advocates censorship and that in the Laws he advocates total censorship— censorship of art, religion and philosophy.)

Thirdly, it isn't the case that communism can't be applied to a non-industrial society (what about Communist China, for example?).

THE JUSTIFICATION FOR ALL THIS: A state is united when most people are happy about the same things, unhappy together about certain other things. What keeps a state from achieving such unity is disagreement over what is to be called "mine" and "thine". In the way that an entire body can feel it when a finger is hurt, so the best-ordered state is unified: if anyone suffers pain, it must be the concern of the whole state.

The people will call the guardians "helpers" (not "masters," as in ordinary states). The guardians will call the people "supporters" and "foster-parents" (not "slaves," as in ordinary states). The guardians will call one another "fellow guardians" and "kinsmen." And they shall also treat one another as kinsmen. In this way, they will have their interests, their pleasures and pains, in common. All this will be the result of the guardians' having a community of wives and children.

Such unity is also promoted by the fact that the guardians have no private property and no pay. As their families are communal, so is their property. There will thus be no strife about "mine" and "thine." No guardian will own something so that his interests might conflict with those of the state. Nor will he ever be prompted to do something merely for gain, since he can gain nothing (being forbidden to own whatever it is he might gain). With no interest apart from the interests of others, there will be a communality of feeling. There will be none of the divisive influences usually introduced by private concerns for one's property or one's children. And if there is nothing to divide them from other men, then the guardians may well feel that *all* older men are their parents, all men of their age their brothers, and all younger men their sons—and thus there will be little likelihood of conflict.

Since they can have no money, there will be no possibility of bribery. Their only reward will be that they are honored as saviors of the country. In Book IV, Adeimantus asked whether these people are not miserable. Does it seem so, now? Their lives will be of the best. No man will want to take over the state and give up this life of happiness.

COMMUNALITY IN WAR: In war, their "sons" shall accompany the guardians—to learn from them, and also to make the fighters fight even harder rather than risk disgrace or defeat in the presence of their "sons." And when the fighters die in battle, they will receive a hero's honor.

In wartime, Plato maintains, no Greek captive should be enslaved (as is now the custom). Nor should Greek territory be despoiled when captured, for Greeks are, after all, united by ties of blood and friendship. (A. E. Taylor, one of the most eminent of Platonic scholars, has determined, on the basis of evidence about the various characters in the dialogue, that the conversation is taking place in 421 B.C., the year in which the Peloponnesian War was interrupted for the Peace of Nicias. Certainly, the words of Socrates would raise a laugh were they uttered at any other time but this: a time when all sensible men were hoping that the peace could be sustained.) When Greeks fight Greeks, let it be called "discord," Socrates says, since they are by nature friends and kinsmen, sharing the same homeland and religion. Let them call it "discord," not "war," since their quarrel will be of the kind that is someday to be reconciled. (This "discord" between Greeks could be bloody enough! See Thucydides' description of the revolution in Corcyraea, in his *Peloponnesian War*, Ch. X.)

ALL THIS IS AN IDEAL: The question of whether this state is possible or only an ideal is answered by Socrates (472 C). We have inquired into all this so that we might have an absolute ideal by which we could judge our own happiness. We are not interested in whether this state can in fact come into existence. Nor are we disturbed that it cannot. When a painter paints the most beautiful figure that he can conceive, the picture is no worse even if there is no living person who conforms to the ideal. The actual fact always falls short of the ideal (473 A). The point, then, in displaying the ideal is to show us how far we actually fall short of it.

THE CAUSE OF EVIL IN STATES: By means of the ideal, we can see one of the great sources of evil in actual states. Our ideal state, we saw, is one in which men are rulers for no reason other than that they possess wisdom. We can see, therefore, that the cause of evil in existing states is that power and wisdom are *not* in the same hands. Those who have power have no real wisdom, and those who know keep away from positions of power. We can therefore say this to all existing states: Until philosophers are kings, or kings have philosophy so that political power and philosophical wisdom are united in the same persons, there will be no end to the evils of this world (473 D).

> **COMMENT:** This is the most famous statement in the *Republic*. (The statement is condensed here.) Plato felt that his experiences with the ruler of Syracuse gave him enough evidence to substantiate this view. (See the discussion of this incident in the last few paragraphs of the Introduction, above.)

WHAT IS A PHILOSOPHER: What is the kind of wisdom so essential to a good state, and for lack of which all the world is in agony? This will have to be determined in subsequent parts of the *Republic*. Here, Socrates merely goes so far as to distinguish his philosopher from the arm-chair scientist, the man who has a bit of curiosity about his world.

A philosopher is not merely a person with a curiosity about something. (See the discussion about the shepherds in the beginning of the Introduction above.) Rather, the philosophers are those who are *lovers* of the vision of truth (475 E). The word "lover" (*philo*-sophia) is to be stressed here: a lover is one who pursues, one who is drawn by beauty. But it is not merely the beauty of a poem or of a person that our philosopher is drawn to. He is drawn, rather, by a desire to find the meaning of beauty in itself, beauty in the abstract.

THE KINDS OF KNOWING: This distinction between, on the one hand, particular instances of beauty and, on the other hand, beauty in and for itself, apart from all particulars, leads Socrates to distinguish different kinds of knowledge. Knowledge of *a* cow named Bossie, *a* dog named Rex, and *a* cat named Melchior would not qualify as knowledge in the sense in which a veterinarian knows *all* cows, *all* dogs, *all* cats. His knowledge is theoretical—involving a grasp of principles—so that he can tell, even *before* he meets Melchior, what kind of diet will produce what kind of general effect. The knowledge of particular things, therefore, is not real knowledge, but mere opinion. True knowledge is not concerned with particular individuals or events, but rather with general principles and the way in which particular things *reflect* those general principles.

Plato offers an ingenious insight here. He will distinguish different faculties, different *ways* of knowing something, in us; and then he will show that for each faculty in us, there is outside us in the world a different level of reality for us to know. Thus, the world corresponds to the apparatus of our thinking, the objective world conforms to our subjective limits. There is a difference between the way in which we conceive of a tree, remember a tree, see an actual tree, or see a tree reflected in water. Each of these acts of ours involves a different faculty in us. And Plato's unique viewpoint is that there is a distinct kind of reality out there for every level of *our* knowing. This is a philosophical position known as Platonic Realism. Some philosophers see it as being similar to Idealism. We shall reserve discussion of it for Plato's treatment of these concepts in later books of the *Republic*.

We must distinguish our faculties of knowing, and find the different kinds of reality corresponding to each. Knowledge is a theoretical grasp of reality, of *being*. Ignorance corresponds to knowing *nothing*. Is there a kind of reality between being and nothing? And is there a kind of knowledge corresponding to this intermediate, unreal reality? Mere opinion is somewhere between knowledge and ignorance. (With mere opinion, I understand my cat, Melchior; but with veterinary knowledge, I understand the principles relating to all cats.) Thus, mere opinion is darker than knowledge, but it is clearer than ignorance (478 C). The object of opinion, that which opinion "knows" about, is somewhere between being and nothing. People who have mere opinion grasp this or that particular thing. But they do not *know*, for knowledge is about absolutes, about principles. The lovers of particulars, then, cannot be knowers, cannot be lovers of wisdom, cannot be philosophers, and so cannot be real rulers. What would be the point of having a ruler who is informed about this particular problem, or even a *set* of particulars? We want a ruler who can have a vision of the totality.

THE REPUBLIC, BOOK VI

It is here that Socrates resumes the discussion that was interrupted in Book IV about the psychological operation of the virtues, the way in which the virtues work in the soul of their possessor. But here he is concerned with the operation of the virtues in the soul of the philosopher. What sort of person is this "lover," this pursuer of wisdom? These questions ultimately lead Socrates to ask, what is the wisdom that is to be pursued? Are there different kinds of wisdom? How do we distinguish the false from the true wisdom?

Socrates ventures a preliminary distinction: philosophers are those who can grasp the eternal and unchangeable. All other men are not philosophers. (The wisdom we aim at is as eternal as $F = MA$ or $E = MC^2$. These formulas might find varying applicability, different kinds of usefulness in different situations. But the truth *to which they refer* is eternal and unchanging.)

The rulers are to be true philosophers. These are the men best fitted for protecting our state. Men who lack this vision of absolute truth are blind, they do not know life's principles, and they do not know what life is for. A man who knows, knows not only the "how" but also the ultimate "why." (Consider the difference between a mechanic who can diagnose the trouble with my car and can fix it, and a scientist who, in addition to being able to fix my car, also knows the principles involved. The scientist will be better able to foresee future difficulties.) If there is to be a choice on the one hand, political "technicians" who lack vision and, on the other hand, those who know the mechanical apparatus of a state *and* have this higher vision in addition, then the choice is obvious (484 D). The difference between technicians (who grasp particular facts) and scientists (who grasp fundamental principles) points to a difference in the kinds of object they are pursuing.

BEING AND BECOMING: The technician is involved in a world of changing particulars, a world in process where nothing is certain or permanent or real, and where no knowledge is possible. This is the world of *Becoming*, and the world of becoming is the world around us. Trees are not fully real for Plato, neither are skyscrapers, people or cats. And we cannot have knowledge of this world, only a cluster of fluctuating opinions.

The scientist, Plato says, is involved in a world of unchanging principles. It is a world that is permanent and certain and real, a world about which we can have true knowledge in terms of eternal laws (such as $A^2 + B^2 = C^2$). This is the world of *Being* (485 B). It is only the scientist (or philosopher) who is concerned with these truths. The mechanic is concerned with how things work here and now. On this basis, he has no real knowledge, since knowledge is concerned only with principles that are always true.

THE FOUR VIRTUES AS THEY WORK IN THE PHILOSOPHER: The difference in pursuit involves a difference in character between two kinds of men: the philosopher's pleasures are the pleasures of the intellect, of the soul, rather than of the body. (This is his use of temperance.) Further, in his role as "spectator of all time and all existence," he cannot be too much concerned with his own life, or fear death. (This is his source of courage.) Nor can such a person be petty or unjust, for how can he be caught up in small things when his primary concern is with the greater? (This is his kind of justice.)

He will take pleasure in knowing; he will have a good memory of what he learns; his soul will be well proportioned. Thus, we find him to be noble, gracious, a friend of truth, justice, courage and temperance (487 A).

Here, Adeimantus voices a feeling that is often expressed by students of Plato. They feel that as they read the dialogue and "agree" with Socrates, point by point, they are not agreeing entirely but are making small concessions, giving in a little on each point—until the conclusion is drawn, and they find that they are disagreeing entirely. This has happened here, Adeimantus says. We have been praising the pursuit of philosophy. Yet the philosophers we know of are either unscrupulous rogues or else they are held to be useless by the world.

THE "USELESSNESS" OF PHILOSOPHERS: Socrates agrees that what Adeimantus says is so. But if they are useless, Adeimantus asks, then how can we say that states will never be rid of evil until philosophers are rulers? Socrates answers with the following parable that speaks volumes about his view of Athenian democracy and its characteristic amateurism.

Some sailors think that they know all about steering a ship. Even though they have never been taught, they maintain that it is the sort of thing every man has a talent for, and that it cannot be taught. Each man considers himself fully capable (of making political decisions). Those sailors get the captain drunk and they take over the ship. Whoever goes along with their mutiny (the democratic politician, responsible to the "people"), is rewarded with the honorific title of "sailor," "pilot" or "able seaman" (as we might call a man who does this in public life, catering to our whims, a "great statesman"). A good pilot, however, must *know* all sorts of things about meteorology (so he can predict what the winds will be) and astronomy (so he can navigate by the stars). How would such a true pilot be treated by the mutineers? Wouldn't they call him a star-gazer and a good-for-nothing?

THE RELATION OF THE TRUE PHILOSOPHER TO THE STATE: We can see from our parable that the answer to Adeimantus is, not that the philosopher is intrinsically useless to the state, but that some states have no use for wisdom, any more than these sailors see the use of a captain. It is true that philosophy is deemed useless but the fault is not the philosopher's. The sailors may not realize that they need a navigator, but that is not the fault of the navigator. Sick people may think they have no need for doctors, but that is not the fault of doctors.

In the same way, we may think we have no need of a man who *knows* how to rule. We may think that this is a talent which all men have. The pay-off is that we ourselves must suffer for our delusion. Thinking that all men have the talent, we choose rulers for all sorts of irrelevant reasons: on the basis of wealth, family or popular appeal. This is as foolish as choosing a doc-

tor because he is tall. No, the only qualification that is relevant
to ruling is the ruler's complete knowledge of what he is doing
—and such knowledge cannot be the mere opinion of the political mechanic. No trial-and-error makeshift will do. The knowledge we need is of the highest level: knowledge of ultimate
Being (490 B).

WHAT MAKES CORRUPT PHILOSOPHERS: If philosophy is so
powerful a force in the shaping of character, how can we
account for the many corrupt philosophers? Socrates answers
strangely: it is often the virtues themselves (courage, temperance, etc.) that corrupt their possessor! (491 B). (It is easy
enough to say that wealth and rank corrupt a man, but how
can virtues corrupt him?) A thoroughbred animal needs greater
care than a mongrel—and suffers more from neglect. When
the most gifted natures, blessed with all kinds of virtues, are
exposed to bad education, they suffer the most. Great crimes,
after all, are not perpetrated by mediocrities but rather by great
natures gone wrong.

What are the influences of corruption? It is not merely the
Sophists, the popular educators, who corrupt the young. It is
also society at large. Whenever people gather in large groups,
whether in congress, in court, or in the theatre, and they
acclaim certain things and disapprove others. What young person can withstand popular opinion? Will he not derive his
notions of good and evil from what the public approves? The
Sophists, the popular educators, do little else than teach what
the multitude of people believe, and thus propagate the pre-
vailing values (493 A).

These educators study the public as though it were a great
beast that must be appeased and controlled. Good or evil are
what the beast takes as good or evil. There is no justification
for these values other than that these are what the beast wants.
Artists and dramatists, too, give the public what it demands
(convincing themselves that whatever the public demands is
good *because* the public demands it). In this sort of environment, is there any place for absolute truth, or absolute beauty?
Obviously not. We must conclude, therefore, that the public is
at heart antagonistic to truth and philosophy. The real philosopher will be condemned by them.

There is another influence tending to corrupt potential philosophers and to keep them away from a life devoted to reason. If young people show any kind of promise, if they display various abilities and virtues, they will be wooed into "successful" careers in public life. It is very difficult for such a person not to give in to ambition. (Is Plato speaking of his own contact with public life, as a young man?)

Suppose that someone attempts to put him wise, and to show him the better path, is our young man likely to listen? Will his friends let him listen to such advice if they see in him one of the eventually "successful" people, one of the slick fish who will make it in this world? They will do almost anything to prevent him from giving in to his better nature. In this way, the outstanding virtues that could make a man a great philosopher are used against him by the world (495A). From this class of outstanding men we are to get the men who can be the most disastrous to mankind—or the most beneficial—and which kind of man they become depends on the education they receive, and the kind of life they choose for themselves.

If the outstanding youths are corrupted who will be left, then, for the practice of philosophy but the mediocrities, attracted by the showy dignity of it all? These men have little to offer but sophisms. Other than these, there are a handful, here and there, devoted to true philosophy because they are fed up with the madness of the multitude and with the corruption of the political world (496 D). A man of this small minority can do little to correct the world, nor will he join its madness. He is content if he can cultivate his own garden and be left in peace. (Strange thoughts from an Athenian, they for whom public life was as natural as breathing.)

HOW OUGHT THE STATE TO PURSUE PHILOSOPHY?: At present, we find philosophy taught to the young, in the period between childhood and the time they enter upon the more "serious" tasks of money-making and housekeeping. What they ought to be doing is exercising their bodies, Socrates says. Only gradually, as they mature, should they be made to exercise their minds as well. But as we have never seen the perfect city, so we have never seen the perfect practice of philosophy. It is for this very reason that we can say that there will never be perfection in cities until true philosophers rule them (499 C).

All this is difficult and improbable, but not impossible. Mankind *can* be educated, if it is done with love (500 A). With our eyes on that which is eternal and unchanging, we can shape a state in accordance with a divine pattern. We must take the existing codes of law and customs, and wipe the slate clean. Then we must draw the bare outline of a new constitution, filling in the details when we have in our sight absolute justice and beauty and temperance, combining all this in an image of man. We will erase here, add a detail there, until we have arrived as closely as possible to divine perfection. By this way of doing it, men will slowly come to see the wisdom of this procedure. (Note that Socrates is not presuming to enact law for all time. His is a method of careful and judicious experiment, but with an eye toward the absolute.) It is not outlandish to imagine that people might be won over to this course of action and be persuaded to follow it, constructing their lives rationally with a view to the good of all, rather than settling for what they have. (Have we not seen the examples of the Mayflower Compact and the Israeli collective "kibbutz"?)

MORE ON THE TRAINING OF RULERS: There will be only a few of them, since the wide range of the talents required are rarely to be found combined in the same person. We have already described his training in lower ranks, involving music and gymnastics. He must also, however, be proficient in knowledge of the highest kind. This sort of knowledge cannot be arrived at by a short cut. He must work at it, like an athlete in training. The circuitous path is necessary because the knowledge he is to attain is higher even than justice and the other virtues (504 D): what he must aim for is the concept that includes all these. (What shall we call such an inclusive concept? Is there a science of it? How can it be known?)

In the way that the concept of "courage" is inclusive of, and more abstract than, particular instances of it such as a soldier's courage or a doctor's courage, so the concept we want now is a concept that is wider than that of the virtues. It is a still higher level of abstraction: the idea of *good*. All other things are good to the extent that they reflect this. This is the knowledge that our philosopher-king must have for it is knowledge of the most universal kind. Without this highest form of knowledge, of what "good" is any other kind of knowledge? How can we know the value of things, therefore, without knowing what value is, in and for itself?

WHAT IS THE HIGHEST VALUE, THE HIGHEST GOOD?: Some people say that the good for the sake of which we do everything else is pleasure. (J. S. Mill, in *Utilitarianism*, for instance. G. E. Moore, in *Principia Ethica* has, however, argued that there are *logical* fallacies imbedded in all such naturalistic philosophies. One of these fallacies involved in equating "pleasure" and "good" is made evident when we substitute one for the other in a sentence. Socrates will show the error of this, below.)

Others, he continues, have maintained that knowledge is the highest good but they cannot explain what they mean by knowledge. Highest good = knowledge. Knowledge of what? They finally fall into the trap of saying that the highest good is a knowledge of good—which would mean that whenever we use the word "good" we mean our knowledge of it. (To say that a pie is good is not the same thing as saying that it is good *because* I know it to be good.)

And if anyone says that pleasure is the highest good, he has to fall into a similar logical error when he admits that there are bad pleasures as well as good ones. (If good = pleasure, and there are bad as well as good pleasures, then there would have to be "bad goods" which is self-contradictory, or "good goods," which is a trivial repetition.)

WHAT OUR RULER MUST KNOW IS THE HIGHEST GOOD: How can he know justice, unless he knows why it is good? But to know why it is good, he must know this highest good. What is this highest good, Adeimantus asks. Is it knowledge or pleasure or neither one? (506 B.) Socrates insists that he cannot get closer to this than an approximation. He can show us only the "child" of the good, not the parent. In other words, he will show us the implications of the idea, its offspring. The idea itself will be approached later.

To begin with, we must see what kind of thing "good" is, so that we may see how it is to be understood. Is "goodness" a thing at all? No, but there are many good things, all sharing the quality "good." These things are seen (a good painting, a good horserace). The quality of "good," however, is not something seen with the eye but rather is something known.

Note that Socrates distinguishes two kinds of reality, corresponding to two faculties of our minds: Paintings are *particular* things; they can be seen. The "goodness" of a painting is not a particular thing, however, but rather a *universal* quality; it cannot be seen but must be understood as a concept. "Goodness" is called a universal quality because it can be shared by many paintings, but only one painting can be this particular painting.

PARTICULARS AND UNIVERSALS: Only particulars are seen by the eye; only universals are understood by the mind. When we see this *painting*, it is not *this* painting that we understand; what we understand about this particular painting are its universal qualities: mood, meaning, form, and so on. Nor do we "see" the concept of form, the concept of color. Concepts are grasped by the intellect, not by the eye. The "good" is such a concept. It cannot be seen by the eye. Nowhere do we visually see "good," as we see this particular patch of yellow (507 B).

Now that we know that there are two kinds of reality (particular things and universal qualities), corresponding to two faculties of mind (seeing and understanding), the question now is: Which is superior to the other? Which is dependent upon the other? Which are more real, things or ideas? Let us see whether sensation needs anything else in order to function.

SEEING IN LIGHT: Seeing has need of something else: light. The eye merely has the passive capacity to see. It sees "by means of" light. Light, alone, is not seeing, rather it is a condition necessary for seeing to take place. Socrates uses the sun as the symbol of light. Now, as the sun is the necessary condition of seeing, so the "good" is the necessary condition of knowing. It is the basis for knowing the value of something. The most basic thing we can know about something is to know its value, and we cannot know value itself except by defining what we mean by good. It follows that we cannot *know* anything at all until we know good. The good is the fundamental concept that underlies all thinking. Just as a concept (for example, form) underlies our understanding of paintings, so a concept of all concepts underlies *them*, and this is the concept of "good." As the sun is the source of the light by which we see, so "good" is the source of the light by which we understand.

"THE SUN": Socrates speaks of the sun as the child of the good, begotten in his likeness. He explains what he means by this analogy: it is the sun that makes things visible to the eye. Now, consider the soul as though it were the eye, an organ of apprehension. Just as the sun makes things visible to the eye, so truth and being make things understandable to the soul. In the dusk, the eye perceives dimly. In the darkness of the world of change and unreality and "becoming," the soul has no knowledge but only opinion. That which makes known things true, and gives knowers the power to know (as the sun gives them power to see) is the idea of "good." Thus, it is the source of all our understanding and science.

As light and sight are *like* the sun but are not the sun, so knowledge and truth are like the "good," but are not identical with the "good." And just as the sun is the source not only of visibility but also of growth, so the idea of "good" is the source not only of knowledge of things but also of their being and essence. And yet, the good is of a still higher essence than all this. These are its "children."

THE DIVIDED LINE (509 D): We have seen that there are two kinds of reality corresponding to two faculties of mind (and two kinds of reliability about our information). How, exactly, do reality and mind correspond? Plato will show us an intricate continuum of reality in the world, so that some things are more *real* than others, in an ascending scale. Then he will show us that our minds have the same kind of continuum, so that some things are more *knowable* than others. And then, he will show that as we go higher in the scale of reality we also go higher in the kind of knowledge.

In order to demonstrate this continuum, he uses a line which he divides in certain unequal proportions. Divide a line into two unequal parts, A and B. Let A, the larger part, stand for the world that can be grasped by the intellect. Let B, the smaller part, stand for the world that can be seen by the senses. Thus:

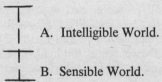

A. Intelligible World.

B. Sensible World.

Now, in the same proportion as A is to B, divide A into A1 and A2, and divide B into B1 and B2. Thus:

LEVELS OF KNOWING			LEVELS OF REALITY
	Reason	A1. Principles, theories	
Knowledge (A)	Understanding by seeing	A2. Mathematical representation	(A) *Being* Intelligible world
Opinion (B)	Belief in particular objects.	B1. Existing things	(B) *Becoming* Sensible world
	Deception, delusion.	B2. Images, reflections	

Let us say that B1 is a globe that I see. B2 is its reflection in a pool of water. Obviously, B2 is not as real as B1. The reflection depends on the original, and it can be disturbed, while the globe continues to exist. The reflection owes its reality to the visible globe.

Now, in the same way that B2 is a copy of B1, perhaps B as a whole is a copy of A as a whole. Perhaps this same sort of dependence exists between the sensible world and the intelligible world. All of B is a mere reflection of intelligible principles (A) that are more real, more knowable. (The reason why Plato uses the proportioned line is to demonstrate a similarity of dependencies.)

The visible globe (B2) could be destroyed. Yet I could still represent the principle of it: $x^2+y^2=z^2$. I could draw diagrams about it, show that certain relations hold between arcs, chords and radii—and that these relations hold of *all* globes, universally. Obviously then these principles are more real than the existing globe, since the principles can outlast it, are true even if no one has yet discovered them, and so on. These principles would hold true even if there were no globes in existence. (We must *not* make the mistake, therefore, of identifying "reality" with "existence." The two are at opposite ends of the line.)

Observe, therefore, that the world of A2, in which I draw my theorems on a blackboard, is not as real as A1, in which I can express my principles purely theoretically, using no visual crutch. In drawing figures (A2), I rely on certain principles without having to explain them. The explanation (A1) is therefore more rational, knowable, universal. Instead of representing a globe as $x^2+y^2=z^2$, I can spell out the definition in terms of: "a solid figure, every point of whose surface is equi-distant from another point, etc." In A2, I can show you *how* to bisect an angle. In A1, I can also explain what I am doing, and what the principles are.

A1 is therefore a higher form of intelligence, as it is a higher level of reality. Here, we no longer use our physical eyes, but the eye of the mind. Thus, there are different degrees of knowing corresponding to different degrees of reality—and for both, whether knowledge or reality, each degree is a mere copy of the degree that is higher, and is dependent upon it for its truth. To extend this analogy further, we must say that the entire world-system—from A1 to B2—is all a mere reflection of a still higher principle; and this is the overarching principle of the good, the "parent" of all that this has shown. This over-arching "good" is somehow God and yet it is not. It is the fundamental rationality of the world, that which makes it obey law (whether the law is natural, mathematical, or human).

THE REPUBLIC, BOOK VII

In the previous book, Socrates discussed two important topics: a) the relation of the philosopher to existing society, and why the philosopher will always be condemned by society; b) the relation between the levels of reality and the various levels of knowledge. It would seem that these two topics have nothing in common. The first is sociological, the second is metaphysical. Finding a unifying context within which to discuss these widely different problems would seem to be impossible. Yet, these two themes are magnificently combined in the present book, in a vividly graphic representation that has come to be known as the Myth of the Cave.

THE MYTH OF THE CAVE: There are men who have lived in a cave ever since childhood. They sit facing the far wall of the cave. Their legs and necks are chained so that they cannot move; they can look only straight ahead of them, at the wall. Behind them, near the mouth of the cave, there is a fire. And between the fire and the prisoners there is a raised walkway with a parapet. Along this walkway, certain other men pass, carrying various kinds of objects: vessels, statues, and so on, made of wood or stone. The fire casts their shadows on the far wall.

Glaucon interrupts by remarking on the strangeness of this situation and these prisoners. And Socrates answers, significantly, that they are very much like ourselves. He wants, from the start, to make this allegory relevant to our own existence. These prisoners see only the shadows of one another since they cannot turn their heads from side to side. (Thus, they never see one another as three-dimensional beings, but only as shadows. Do they, perhaps, think of *themselves* as shadows since they have never seen anything but two-dimensional shapes?)

Now, the prisoners can speak with one another, and they give names to what they see on the wall. There is an echo in the cave, so that whenever one of the men on the parapet speaks, the prisoners imagine that his voice is coming from the shadow on the wall. These talking shadows, then, are reality for the prisoners. The statues being carried by the men on the parapet are mere images, but the shadows cast by these are even less real, being images of images. (This is level B2—see the Divided Line in Book VI.)

WHAT HAPPENS TO A PRISONER WHEN LIBERATED?: If he is made to stand up, turn around, and look at the light, the sudden glare will give him great pain, so that he must shut his eyes. He can no longer see the shadows, the so-called "realities," and is completely unable to function. Suppose we tell him that these shadows he thinks to be real are illusions, and that he will now be able to grasp the true reality. We show him the real objects as they pass before him—but they mean nothing to him. He still thinks the shadows to be more real. If we try to bring home the truth to him by making him look directly at the fire, he will turn his head away and look to the more comfortable shadows; these shadows will be "clearer" to him.

Suppose, however, that we drag him up the rugged slope into the daylight. Now he is almost blinded. After a lifetime of "seeing" in darkness, he is now unable to see anything at all. He will have to adjust himself slowly to this upper world. First, he will look at the shadows and the reflections of things (B2); then, when he can bear this, he will look at the objects themselves (B1). He will see that they have color and three-dimensionality, where he saw only two-dimensional patches of gray before.

He is growing accustomed to the light. He can look at the stars, and at the moon (A2) which merely reflects the light of the sun. Only after a long time, however, will he be able to look directly at the sun (beyond A), and no mere reflection of it. He will see it in its proper place and as it really is. Then he will be able to see that it is the sun that is the source of all the things he sees. And he will realize, also, that in a very indirect way, the sun is also the cause of the fire and of the shadows in the cave.

WHAT ABOUT THE OTHER PRISONERS?:   He will pity them, of course, now that he knows that they are living in a complete delusion (B2). They do not know the depth of their error, let alone that they are in error at all. They go on their way, giving prizes and positions to prisoners who are good at telling the difference between one kind of shadow and another. Our liberated philosopher would now find the old life impossible. Despite all the riches, honors and established lore of that old world, he can no longer believe in its "realities."

HE FEELS COMPELLED TO LIBERATE THE OTHERS: He goes back into the cave, but this time he is completely helpless. He cannot see at all, and so he cannot compete in the pursuits which the prisoners regard as highly important: becoming expert at shadow-telling, devoting a lifetime to the study of one kind of shadow, transmitting these scraps of "knowledge" (opinion) to others, and so on. They are the "successful" ones; they have never left the darkness. Compared to them, our philosopher—his eyes still full of the sun—is utterly inept among them. Men laugh at him for having made the terrible trip to the upper world for nothing. They even resolve to learn from his example, and they declare that if anyone ever liberates another and takes him up to the light they will kill him.

THE MEANING OF THE ALLEGORY: Socrates expressly relates the myth to his discussion of the Divided Line in Book VI. The cave is the world of sensations, opinion, change and becoming (B), while the world outside the cave is the intelligible world of knowledge, eternal truth and permanent Being (A). The journey upwards is, of course, the ascent of the soul into enlightenment. The journey ends with a direct sight of the sun, the idea of "good"—that which Socrates holds to be the most fundamental concept of all science since it is the concept that explains the world's law-like rationality. Although it is fundamental to science and the most basic of things to ask about, it is seen last of all, and then only after great effort.

COMMENT: If our philosopher had succeeded in freeing one of the prisoners, he would no doubt have led him out quickly, since he knew the way. But this would be a mistake. The first time up, our philosopher must have stumbled about in his blindness and bruised his knees. He would have had to adjust himself very carefully to the light, trying various things to look at, and suffering when he looked at the light too soon. Now that he knows the dangers, he guides the prisoner. But this process of adjustment is not something you can go through for someone else; no one can be led by the hand, each must do his own stumbling. This is one reason why Plato and Socrates insist on dialogue rather than simply *telling* us what they believe. In being told, we are told other people's beliefs. These do not convince as do conversation: here we can do our own stumbling; but this is the only way to grasp what the sun really means, when we finally see it.

When we finally see the sun, we see it to be the "parent" of all light, the source of all meaning—"the universal author of all things beautiful and right, parent of light and of the lord of light in this visible world, and the immediate source of reason and truth in the intellectual [world]" (517 C). It is knowledge of this sort that our rulers must have.

THE "BLINDNESS" OF PHILOSOPHERS: The allegory also explains why our philosophers are "useless" in this world: they are blinded either by going into the light or else in coming back from the light into darkness. The first kind of blindness is to be envied, the second pitied. Extending the analogy, Socrates says we are wrong to think we can put knowledge *into* a soul. This is as impossible as putting sight into blind eyes. Rather, the capacity to know is in the soul already; it merely needs to be guided, "turned" to the light. (The term "conversion," in the religious sense, means "turning to.") The point of emphasis is that this turning must be gradual. The eye must become accustomed to *endure* light, as the soul must learn to endure its contact with true Being and the good. Without a knowledge of value, mere intelligence can as easily turn us towards crime as towards virtue (519 A).

THE PRIMARY OBLIGATION OF OUR RULERS: In our state, we will prepare our rulers, from earliest childhood, to be capable of making the climb. And then they must be made to return to the cave afterwards, and work among the prisoners (519 D). This is their primary responsibility. (Plato can feel justified in opening a school rather than going back into the political "cave" of Athens. But that is because he is living in a state in which there is no "use" for the philosopher. In the *Republic*, however, the philosopher's place is the political world.)

It might appear unjust to force them back into the cave when they could obviously be happier outside. But it is not the happiness of one class we are aiming for, but rather the happiness of the entire state. It is for the sake of that larger happiness, then, that they must return. In other states, philosophers grow by their own efforts and owe nothing to society. But in our state, we have exposed them to enlightenment so that they might make proper rulers. They must therefore return to the cave and learn to live in it once more; they must learn to see in the dark (520 C). Once they can see again, they will see better than any of the prisoners who never left the cave. The shadows will be the same, but the philosophers will know the reality which these shadows represent. They will not make the mistake of believing the shadows to be the ultimate reality. When men know that the shadows are mere shadows, they will no longer fight over them as they now do in their struggle for power. Once they see that power has little to offer, they will no longer be eager to serve. Indeed, it is a measure of a good state that the public officials are reluctant to serve, and it is a mark of the corruption of a state that they are eager to serve.

HOW ARE SUCH GUARDIANS TO BE PRODUCED? (521 C): How are they to be brought from darkness to light? How is this "conversion" to take place? First, we must ask what sort of knowledge it is that has the power to draw the soul from the world of change and becoming (B) to the world of reality and Being (A). Music and gymnastics are inadequate here, since these might give us a psychological harmony but no science or knowledge. The only other thing is mathematics, since it is common to arts, sciences, and to the uses of intelligence in general. Mathematics, if anything, can draw the soul toward higher reality. It is this discipline alone which shows us how to find the universal concepts in our sense-experience (523 C).

THE SUPREME VALUE OF MATHEMATICS: We might see two chairs and three tables, and say that we therefore see five pieces of furniture. But all that is actually seen are individual chairs and tables. The "two," "three," "five," even the "and" that puts them together, are not seen by the eye. Nobody has ever seen a "two" by itself, nor an "and" either. (We have seen the symbols of them, of course, but what we are talking about are not the symbols but the concepts they represent.) We are dealing with universal concepts here, not visual ones. And mathematics helps to get us out of the sensory-world (B) into the world of thought (A).

MATHEMATICAL CONFUSIONS LEAD THE MIND UPWARDS: Socrates shows us how the eye, if we trusted it, could see both the qualities of "large" and of "small" in the same object. When the senses perplex us with contradictory information, we call upon intelligence to explain, and to make distinctions not found in the world of sense-experience. In the same way, also, our study of mathematics leads us into conflict with the sensory world, into contradictions which can be resolved only by an exercise of mind. And that is the way mathematics stimulates thought.

We are led, for example, to consider ultimate questions such as: "What is unity?" (That is, we are led to ask these questions if we give full play to our human curiosity. One could, of course, spend a lifetime in mathematics without wondering about such things. But what value is there to a life in which we never ask questions, never go beneath the surface of things? "The unexamined life is not worth living," is Socrates' famous remark before the court, in the dialogue entitled *Apology.* The basis of something as "obvious" and commonplace as arithmetic has, in recent times, been re-examined in a very exciting way, and shown to be filled with controversial questions. There are untold perplexities in answering the question, "What is number?" See G. Frege, *Foundations of Arithmetic.*)

Glaucon himself gives us an example of the examination of the obvious—the systematic curiosity about ultimates—that is the whole point of philosophy: When we ask what "one" is, we find that it is both a unity as well as an infinite set of fractions (525 A). Thus, it is both, "one" and "many." How can this be? It is perplexities such as these that lead us onto higher levels of analysis and thought. Our philosophers, then, must know mathematics—not on the level of A2, where we perform certain procedures mechanically, bisecting angles or using numbers without knowledge of the principles involved, but on the level of A1, where the nature of number is known by our reason. In this way, the soul is lead upwards to study higher and still higher principles, leading to a knowledge of the eternal, the sun itself.

THE USEFULNESS OF MATHEMATICS:	In addition to number, our rulers are also to study geometry and astronomy. These will be useful also in war. Socrates is amused at Glaucon's insistence on justifying these in terms of their "usefulness." We could bring in all of Socrates' earlier criticism of what society finds "useful," and his comment on how self-destructive society is in finding the philosopher "useless." In the light of all the foolishness perpetrated in history, the multitude of men are very poor judges of what is "useful" to themselves. If they were good judges of "usefulness," society would have resolved its difficulties long ago. In his state, Socrates says, research into solid geometry, of which very little is known, would be subsidized by the state, since such study would have the highest kind of "usefulness"—the enlightenment of the rulers.

THE STUDY OF MUSIC:	In all our studies, we have emphasized the importance of getting away from sensory elements (A2) and approaching pure principles (A1). Musical harmony, too, must be studied for its mathematical relations. The Pythagoreans, whom Socrates mentions, were a group devoted to mystical and mathematical studies around the late sixth to the late fourth centuries B.C. For them, the underlying substances of all things were numbers and mathematical relations. They were the first to discover the connection between music and mathematics. They measured the lengths of a vibrating string for each note, and they found that an interval of an octave involved a relation of two to one, e.g., twenty inches to ten inches. In our terms, we would say that the two notes, let us say the middle A and the high A, vibrate at 440 and 880 cycles per second. (Why do the two A's vibrate at 440 and 880, rather than at 447.333 and 876.2666. . . .?) This Pythagorean discovery, that all the intervals in music involve relations of whole integers, not irrational fractions, was one of the first intimations of the law-like rationality of the world. Socrates would condemn this study of harmony as being on the level of A2. What the Pythagoreans never explain is *why* certain combinations are harmonious while others are not.

DIALECTIC: The true "usefulness" of all these studies becomes evident when they are unified and inter-related. This would obviously be an enormous task. Yet all this is a mere prelude to a still higher study: that of reasoning itself. Socrates calls this "dialectic" (532 A). He means not only logic, which is what the term dialectic means, in Greek, but also all of metaphysics and epistemology—the studies, respectively, of the underlying basis of reality and of the nature of knowledge.

All the other sciences, concerned with producing and constructing, leave their presuppositions unexamined. Dialectic alone undertakes to examine these first principles as well. The sciences rest on hypotheses. Dialectic eliminates hypotheses, replacing them with secure foundations (533 C). Thus, dialectic is more fundamental than any of the sciences and is also their corrective. The role of philosophy, then, is seen here as critic of the sciences.

ON WHAT LEVEL OF KNOWLEDGE IS SCIENCE? Without adequate justification for its underlying assumptions, and most of these assumptions are never even made explicit, let alone justified, the sciences occupy an intermediate position. They are somewhat higher than mere opinion (B), but lower than pure reason (A1) in which we can fully justify our beliefs by means of principles, and then justify those principles by means of higher reasoning. The actual place of science, then, is the "understanding" (A2) wherein I can understand the use of certain operations, such as bisecting an angle, without being able to give an adequate reason for my methods.

The purpose of dialectic is to arrive at the reasoned grasp of the essences (or universal qualities) of things (534 B). Beyond this, the ultimate aim is the essential grasp of "good" itself, to attain knowledge of absolute Being (537 D).

CONCLUDING REMARKS BY SOCRATES: Socrates follows all this with a review of the characteristic traits of the philosopher-kings. To this is added a review, with some further detail, of the educational methods to be used. He changes his mind about his earlier view that the highest training ought to be given only to old men. Let mathematics be taught to children—but without any sort of compulsion. The body can be trained under compulsion but the mind cannot. Let education, therefore, be given to children as an amusement.

Let them also be exposed to the widest range of experience. Let them be taken into battle so that they may see what it is! (In our time, we romanticize battle on TV, and the child may grow up with an eagerness for it. Were he to see real men killed, he might have a more judicious hesitation about war, later on in life.)

The age at which they can begin to unify their knowledge into a comprehensive dialectic is 30. There is a danger here, when one kind of knowledge is replaced by another. Imagine a young man who suddenly finds that the people he thought were his parents are only his foster-parents. Who his true parents are, he does not yet know. Will he not be less obedient and less respectful to his foster-parents? By the same reasoning, will he not, when he studies the new sciences, be less respectful of his earlier knowledge and be less obedient to his earlier loyalties to moral and political codes; will he not go into a confusion that is typical of many students who feel that nothing is real, all is relative and who therefore argue for the sake of arguing?

THE REPUBLIC, BOOK VIII

Here we have Plato's theory of history. His theory combines two themes already familiar to us: (1) the identification of the state with the individual, (2) the concept that all change is a deterioration. What is unique in Plato's treatment is the way these two themes are combined. First, however, let us discuss them separately, as his psychological and his metaphysical interpretations of history. These are only elements, however. They must be seen as parts of one grand psychological-metaphysical theory of history.

THE PSYCHOLOGICAL INTERPRETATION OF HISTORY: Plato will treat states and individuals in the same terms. His justification for this procedure is two-fold: states are composed of individuals, so that whatever destroys individuals will also destroy the state they are a part of; further, it is possible to consider individual souls as though they were governments with problems about what part shall rule, and so on.

The forces of change ought therefore to be the same for states as for individuals. That which makes a state deteriorate from a timocracy to an oligarchy, and then to a democracy, is the same cluster of circumstances that makes a timocratic (honor-seeking) father have an oligarchic (money-seeking) son, and then makes such a money-hungry individual have a libertine for a son. Socrates will therefore consider the four types of bad state: timocracy, oligarchy, democracy, and tyranny. And after each of these discussions about a specific type of state, he will talk about the relevant type of individual character: the timocratic man, the oligarchic man and so on. He will follow through with this parallelism in a very imaginative way, and at every turn we might find caricatures of ourselves—for instance, societies that begin with a dream of idealistic equality and end up being ruled by a small-time thug whom they cannot shake off. And always, the fault is in ourselves and in the sort of individuals we are. The deterioration of states begins in the seeds of self-destruction imbedded in the souls of individual men. And always, the process of historical change is a downhill one. Why? This is answered by the other half of Plato's theory of history.

THE METAPHYSICAL INTERPRETATION OF HISTORY: We saw, at the end of Book VI, that the world of reality and Being (A) is separate from the world of change and becoming (B). It was pointed out, in our discussion of it, that "reality" does not mean the same as "existence." The most real kind of state, after all, does not exist. The concept of a circle is more real than any existing circle, since the concept would be eternal and real even if no circles were to exist. And existing circles (existing in time) can rust or warp or fall to pieces. Indeed, they *must* do so eventually. But of the *concept* of the circle it is timelessly true that the area of a sector is equal to $\frac{1}{2}r^2\theta$. And this is true of circles even before this truth is discovered by mathematicians.

Reality and existence are therefore at opposite ends of the Divided Line. That which exists in time is undergoing change. It is therefore unreal, since that which is real is outside time altogether. This means that history, a process in time, cannot be a process headed for reality. Whatever is real must be eternally real, timelessly real. Whatever is in time is headed in the direction of unreality: it is destined for decay. All history is therefore a story of deterioration. All history is downhill. The theory of evolution says that history is a development of forms, a process upwards. For Plato, "forms" can only be eternal, so history is a process downwards. The perfect state will have no history—unless it is dying, and is no longer a true Republic. Only the four bad states will have a history, and that history is a view of society in terms of its illnesses, not its possibilities for health. Plato's theory of history is therefore a pathology of states.

SOCRATES' DISCUSSION OF THE FOUR TYPES: At the end of Book IV and the start of Book V, Socrates had said that there is only one form of true wisdom. The forms of evil, however, are many; but he had selected four types as being the most characteristic of injustice in the state and soul. At the start of Book V, this line of argument had been interrupted for the discussion about the training of women, and so on. Here, in Book VIII, he resumes the discussion of the four kinds of false states and evil souls.

The four false types of government are: timocracy, oligarchy democracy, and tyranny. But there are as many forms as there are forms of men's character. The best, we have already seen, is the rule by the men who are best. The traditional Greek term "aristocracy" means "rule by the best." But obviously the traditional meaning is not the same as the literal meaning. Socrates uses the term literally, since rule by the best must mean rule by those who are best at ruling, and these can only be the wisest. Socrates repeats his aim in this discussion: it is to find the form which is most conducive to happiness, to show that Thrasymachus was wrong when he said that a life of injustice was the best kind of life.

THE TIMOCRATIC STATE (545 C): How does it arise in the first place? Since all process is deterioration, this form of government must be a come-down from something better. What is better is our Republic, an aristocracy of intellect. This is a perfectly united state, and such a state cannot change. How, then, does it deteriorate into a timocracy? As it is stated here, the problem is insoluble in its own terms. If it cannot change, then how does it happen that it *does* change? All change, he says, occurs because of a division in the power-structure. From the resulting tension, change comes about. What is this division? In the timocratic state, it is a conflict between the higher and lower factors within it, that is, between the aristocratic and the oligarchic elements.

THE NUMEROLOGICAL PARODY (546 A):   Plato resorts to a dazzling take-off on mathematics. He is not side-stepping the issue. What he is trying to do is to describe a conflict where none can occur. The conflict must be entirely mythical, therefore, and putting it on the level of this whirlwind of numbers makes it almost palatable. This attempt at extracting a literal meaning from numbers is the kind of numerological flim-flam that was practiced by the Pythagoreans. It is so alien to Plato's way of thinking that, here in Book VIII, it comes as a kind of comic relief. Yet it is not altogether alien to him, since he is a mathematician. The difference is that Plato sees mathematics as only one level of reality (A2), and not the highest. For the Pythagoreans, number is *all* reality. Plato plays along with this: he is out-Pythagoreanizing the Pythagoreans. He goes so far as to talk of something like the selection of mates by computer, an idea that has some currency today. For Plato, this is all parody. Perhaps it is even a parody of the *Republic* itself—taking social engineering to its extremes.

THE METALS: One reason why we can see the foregoing episode as a parody of the *Republic* is that Plato uses the analogy of a society divided into the gold, silver, brass, and iron elements. This is an echo of the Noble Lie which is told to the populace earlier on (see Book III, 414 C). He uses this analogy in order to describe the clash between the higher and lower elements in the timocratic state. The timocracy is a state that is ambitious. It is a "government of honors." The iron and brass men are ambitious for money and real estate. The gold and silver admire honor and tradition. The timocracy, therefore, combines the ambition of inferior men with the honor of the gold. Thus, a timocracy is a mixture of good and evil. It is somewhere below the aristocracy of the Republic (gold), yet is above an oligarchy (brass).

The characteristics it takes from aristocracy are the honor given to rulers, their abstention from agriculture and trade, their having meals in common, and the emphasis on gymnastics and military training. This is the system in Sparta, and Plato seems to admire it. Yet he is quick to point out that this is not a true "aristocracy" (rule of the best) since it excludes philosophers from power. A characteristic which the timocracy will share with oligarchy is its pursuit of money (which is not a trait of the aristocrats in the *Republic*). This is what comes of emphasizing gymnastics over music. The soul is not in harmony, the passionate element comes forward, leading to a spirit of ambition and personal conflict.

THE TIMOCRATIC MAN (548 D):   He is self-assertive, a good hunter but a bad speaker. He is rough with servants, not like a cultivated man. He respects power and position (and perhaps justifies them in terms of one another). He claims the right to his own position on the basis of his own feats of arms.

What about the son of such a father? He wants no part of the trouble of living up to this sort of image. He hears his mother complain that his father has not achieved his proper station in life: he is too reserved in some things, people take advantage of his good nature, he is not all man. The son is told that he must be a better man than his father, he must have more in the way of position and wealth. This causes a further deterioration of the state, and results in an oligarchy.

THE OLIGARCHIC STATE (550 C):   The term "oligarchy" literally means "government by the few." Plato is using the term in its conventional sense, to mean "government by the rich." (The proper term for this is "plutocracy.") Our young man has been taught to associate power with money, with each justifying the other. This, then, is a form of government resting on property: the richer a man is, the greater his power.

What ruined the timocracy was the accumulation of wealth. It became the justification for everything else, and was even above the law. Thus, the rivalry for honor (timocracy) gave way to a rivalry for wealth (oligarchy). In the timocracy, power was derived from military valor. In the oligarchy, power comes from money. As the pursuit of riches grows, the pursuit of virtue declines. The figure to be emulated is the rich man, and it is he that is chosen to rule. Ultimately, money becomes a qualification for citizenship and the right to partake in political activity.

The primary weakness of an oligarchy can be seen if we imagine what it would be like to choose the pilot of a ship on the basis of wealth rather than of ability. This applies to all governments when the qualification for rule is anything other than ability: shipwreck! Another weakness is the internal division: such a state is really two states, the rich and the poor, and they are always against each other. The rich are afraid to arm the multitude, even in war. There are extremes of wealth and poverty, and neither man is a true ruler nor a true subject. When wealth is the main goal, we usually find many paupers and criminals in a society. Society becomes polarized: everyone who is not a ruler is miserably poor (typical in Latin-American banana-republics).

THE OLIGARCHIC MAN (553 A): The son of the timocratic man might have seen his father lose his position, suddenly, perhaps by being conspired against. With everything lost, the son decides that the only thing of value is money. The son therefore devotes his energies to this. Money becomes his king and god, and reason and ambition are made secondary. Reason is used only in the service of money-making, ambition comes to admire nothing but the wealthy man. Thus, it is only too easy for an ambitious young man to become an avaricious one and to reject the desire for fame, honor, and love, and limit his ambition to acquiring the one thing that will buy him everything else.

This state, like the man, measures everything in terms of profit. Such a man is always looking to save a penny, and even makes his own purse in order to avoid buying one. Consider what such a man would be like if he had the guardianship of an orphan (the novels of Dickens are filled with such characters). The oligarchic man might even seek respect, but if he does so, it is only in order to safeguard his fortune. Like the state, the man will not be at peace with himself: he will be two men and these will be antagonistic to each other, one part of him will be ambitious for more wealth, the other will be afraid to risk what he has. He is both rich and miserly, and this is a lifelong tension he can never resolve in himself.

THE DEMOCRATIC STATE (555 B): How does the change come about from oligarchy to democracy? In the highly competitive oligarchic states, many young men lose their inherited fortunes before they learn the dangerous ins and outs of business. This makes for a class of embittered, ambitious, but impoverished men. They are without citizenship or a political role since money is the necessary qualification for these things. Such men have little to lose in a revolution, for they no longer have the luxury and idleness they were used to. The cultivation of virtue means little if anything. They only think, "What is to stop me from taking what I want?"

Another way in which democracy comes into being is this: whenever the oligarchy is at war, one party in the state may ally itself with the enemy against the other party. Democracy comes into being when the poor have slaughtered their opponents, the rich. Now every man is considered equal in freedom and power, and judges are chosen by lot (not by vote, which is selective and thus not democratic enough).

Every man is free, and this would seem to be the best of states, the most diversified. But in this diversity is a great danger: no man is governed unless he chooses to be, no man goes into battle unless he chooses to, no man need be excluded from any goal he fancies for himself. No man cares a rap about restricting another; indeed, no man cares about another at all. No one cares to find the proper statesman since no one cares enough about the state. It is, Plato says, "a charming form of government, full of variety and disorder."

THE DEMOCRATIC MAN (558 C):   He is the son of an oligarchic, miserly father who restricted all pleasures that were not deemed strictly "necessary." But such a young man will rebel against restrictions of this kind, and will pursue all the refinements of pleasure. As we saw in the state, one faction can ally itself with a foreign enemy against another faction within the state; so, in the soul of our "democratic" individual, external influences are used to play off one kind of desire against another. His father tells him this-and-this, his friends tell him that-and-that. He is torn in two directions; he is at war with himself. He does not know how to handle these conflicting drives. They are like invaders surrounding a city (Plato draws a fascinating sketch of all this).

Finally, his friends win out; it is their values that take over. He gives himself up to a life of self-indulgence and dissipation "in the country of the lotus-eaters." By this time, all the exertions on the part of his father are useless, for the young man has redefined his values. Modesty and temperance are now rejected as silly and unmanly. Along come anarchy and arrogance, which now are called "freedom" and "style." He now goes from one "kick" to another, letting anything rule him. (He is like the child desperately eager for someone to restrain him, and lashing out at the world because no one will.) He no longer discriminates between good and evil pleasures. His one effort in life seems to be to avoid good advice and common sense. He takes up one fad after another, whether drinking, dieting, sports, business, politics, or even philosophy. It is all done on the spur of the moment. This he regards as a life of pleasure and freedom, and the irony is that many an individual will take such a person as a model to be imitated (whether these models be the decadent Athenians or the jet-set on the Via Veneto).

THE TYRANNICAL STATE (562 A): As democracy comes out of oligarchy, so tyranny comes out of democracy. (Note that democracy is the form of government that is closest to tyranny for Plato. On the basis of his principles, any change in a democracy would be in the direction of tyranny.) It is the pursuit of pleasure and licentiousness (or "freedom" from restraint) that ruins the democracy. This "freedom" is taken as democracy's most glorious trait. Unless the leaders of a democracy indulge the widest possible demands for freedom, the people call them "oligarchs." Thus, under such indulgence, under such absolute freedom, rulers are no better than subjects and subjects are rulers. No one is especially respected or heeded; young and old are treated alike, and the old curry favor with the young. There is immediate reaction against any kind of authority, or restraint, or even law.

The extreme of anything leads to a reaction in the opposite direction: extremes of liberty lead to extremes in slavery. The idlers, the wasters, the drones now take over the hive. In the conflict between the rich and the poor, the middle-class is squeezed dry: each side accuses the middle-class of being loyal to the other.

The mob sets up a tyrant to champion their cause—the man on horseback. First, he is called a protector. But when he has the mob in his hands he can do what he likes with them: killing without trial, redistributing or confiscating property. He knows, however, that he is in danger and so he has some "body-guards," and with this additional power he is an absolute tyrant. At first, he was the "friend of the people," but now he is their "leader." He keeps them in line by fomenting wars, inventing the threat of external enemies so that the people feel they need a strong leader. When he has impoverished them, they depend on him more than ever for their daily needs, and are then far from likely to want to get rid of him. If some individual speaks of freedom he is called an "enemy of the people." With all these wars, the leader eventually makes himself unpopular. He must therefore get rid of anyone who is even likely to be an "enemy," anyone with outstanding qualities of good sense or leadership. He wants only satellites around him, not individuals. Eventually, he makes an enemy of everyone. But if the people want to drive him out they are by now too weak to do so. They wake up one morning to realize that they are enslaved. And thus, liberty has passed into slavery.

The discussion of the tyrannical man will be reserved for Book IX.

THE REPUBLIC, BOOK IX

Earlier, we made the point that Plato's theory of history sees historical change as a symptom of political illness. (The perfect state, being perfectly healthy, will have no history.) His theory of history is therefore a description of the inevitable course of political disease—a pathology of states. Here in Book IX, this illness is to be seen in its most virulent form: the tyranny is the sickest state of all. An entire book is devoted to the tyrannical man because he is, after all, the test case as to whether the life of injustice is better, more natural and happier, as Thrasymachus had claimed. Plato will extend the analogy of health to the individual as well as to states by saying that asking whether justice or injustice is better is like asking whether health or illness is better. That is the substance of his reply to Thrasymachus, a reply supported by some interesting "proofs" and by a unique theory of pleasure.

HOW IS THE TYRANNICAL MAN FORMED FROM THE DEMO-CRATIC?: Something must be said first about desires and appetites. We all may appear to have the neurotic appetites which Socrates calls unlawful ("Those appetites which are awake when reason sleeps," the wild beast capable of incest, sodomy, parricide, and so on), but most of us are successful in keeping these appetites under control. We control these impulses by leading a life of moderation and thought. In practicing moderation, our passions are given their safely measured expression. And in leading a life of thought, we train our reasoning faculty to control the entire psyche. The point which Socrates especially emphasizes is that the beast lives in us all, even in the best of us.

The "democratic" man, it will be recalled, over-reacted against his father's restrictions. He did not, however, give himself altogether to debauchery. Consequently, the two sides of his nature were warring within him. Now, what about the son of this democratic man? Again, there is a conflict, for his father (now more sober) tells him one thing, his friends another. His friends (the "tyrant-makers"), or the lower elements in this conflict that is going on within him, implant in him a monumental passion (573 A). (If we imagine that they get him addicted to drugs, then the rest of Socrates' picture of him fits perfectly.)

TYRANNY AND MADNESS: The passion they implant in him has Madness as its captain. It is the tyrant that rules him, and it rejects all influences such as moderation or shame. There are other examples of such tyrannizing: love, drunkenness, insanity. (When Socrates speaks of "love" here, he is using the word "eros" which means physical lust. The Greeks had a term to distinguish this from the other levels of "love." We have only the one term for both. In the context of this discussion, we are to take the word "eros" as representing all kinds of addiction or tyranny.) Eros imposes demands, that which the addict calls his "habit," and these demands *must* be met. Eros is a tyrant, and will accept no excuses. If our young man has spent all his money, he will defraud his family, even steal from them.

In his "democratic" days, he was still subject to some sort of restraint; he had certain values, certain ways of distinguishing good from evil. But all this is gone now in his "tyrannical" days. Now, he would not stop at murder, nor at any other act, when the tyrant within him commands it.

THE MAN WHO IS HIS OWN TYRANT: The evils done to us by others are as nothing compared with the evils we can inflict on ourselves. Socrates shows this by detailing the crimes which a group of unemployed mercenaries can perpetrate. They choose one from among themselves to be the tyrant, and the crimes he can now commit make theirs seem small. In the same way, the man who is a tyrant over himself can do himself far greater harm than others can do him.

Such men are either masters or servants of others, never friends of anybody. One thing the tyrant (or addict) can never know is true freedom or friendship. Others may admire him but he is really miserable. And since the man is like the state, we can say that such a state is miserable as well. Indeed, if we make a scale from happiness to misery, then the philosopher-king of the Republic (here referred to simply as "king," but Socrates does not mean a conventional monarch) must be the happiest, and the tyrant must be the most miserable and tormented. Socrates offers three proofs for this.

FIRST PROOF OF THE TYRANT'S MISERY (577 C): Socrates makes use of the state-soul analogy. As the tyrannical state is enslaved by a tyrant, so is the tyrannical man enslaved: that which rules in him is the worst in him and is the most insane part. It is ironic that such a man has a slave's soul, not the soul of a free man; he is at the beck and call of all his impulses.

It would seem, therefore, that the tyrannical individual is the most miserable of men. But there is one who is even more miserable: he is the actual tyrant in a state! He has a tyrant within him but he is also unfortunate enough to be a tyrant to others. We might think that he has his slaves under his control. But this control is not a condition of true loyalty on their part. Imagine such a man shipwrecked on a desert island with these "slaves" of his. Would they remain his slaves for long? In the same way, as soon as the tyrant shows weakness there is no one to stand by him.

He is therefore doubly miserable: first, because he has a tyrant within him, and second, because he can hardly be an effective master over others when he cannot be the master of himself. He himself is the worst slave he owns, for he has desires which he can never shake off. He has more needs than anybody, so he is more dependent than anyone and actually poorer than anyone. Like the state he lives in, he is filled with fears. And, worst of all, power does not help him. It only makes him worse off: he becomes more frightened, more ruthless, more alone than ever. (Compare the last months of Hitler and Stalin.)

SECOND PROOF OF THE TYRANT'S MISERY (580 D): Here, Socrates makes use of his division of the soul. As there were seen to be three faculties: reason, spirit (or will), and desire (or sensation) let us speak of a certain kind of man corresponding to each: lovers of wisdom, lovers of honor, and lovers of gain. Which of these has the best kind of life, and which has the worst? Before we can answer this, we must determine which one of the three is in the best position to decide.

The lover of wisdom must be the judge, since he alone can have had experience of all three kinds of pleasures. Lest it appear that Socrates is stacking the deck in his favor, let us realize that the lover of gain could not possibly know what the pleasures of wisdom are—or he would no longer be a lover of gain. Of course, all three men might know honor when they succeed in their aims. But only the philosopher, the "lover of wisdom," literally, knows his own love and all the others. Further, the other lovers have not had enough experience in exercising their judgment, so they would not make good judges, *per se*. Who is the best judge except he who has had experience in the use of the faculty devoted to judgment—reason? We must therefore abide by the judgment that the life of reason is the most pleasant. After this comes the pursuit of honor. And last of all comes the pursuit of gain and the indulgence of the appetites—the basic characteristic of the tyrant and the tyrannical man.

THIRD PROOF OF THE TYRANT'S MISERY (583) B): Here, Socrates speaks of the *reality* of the various pleasures. Pleasure is the opposite of pain, it is said. But there is a neutral condition: when we are sick, health seems to be the highest of pleasures. Yet a healthy person is not aware of his health as a pleasurable state. Nor is the absence of pain in itself a pleasurable state. While I have a headache, the thought of being without it seems like a pleasure. But right now I have no headache, and I cannot say that the no-headache is a pleasure I am feeling. The absence of pain is not, after all, a positive sensation such as a tickle. This neutral state is looked to as a pleasure, therefore, only while we *are* in pain, not while we are in the neutral state. In the same way, the neutral state looms as something painful while we are in a pleasurable state and do not want the pleasure to end.

Thus, the neutral state is seen both as pleasurable and as painful. But can that which is neither pleasure nor pain become both? Pleasures and pains are motions or activities of the soul. The neutral state, however, is one of rest, not of activity.

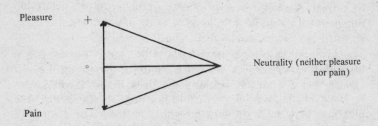

The absence of pain is not pleasure, but is a neutral state. And the absence of pleasure is not pain, but is a neutral state. The absence of activity is not in itself an activity, but is the neutral state of inactivity. For Epicureanism, a later philosophy, pleasure is the absence of pain: the path away from pain is the same as the path toward pleasure. But there are pleasures which do not replace pain, nor are they replaced by pain. Think of the pleasure of smelling roses; it is not painful to stop, only neutral—it is the absence of pleasure, not the opposite of pleasure. So the path away from pain is not identical with the path to pleasure. (For Freud, pleasure and pain are quite close, often interchangeable; they form one continuum, and the opposite of *this* is neutrality.)

THE UNREALITY OF SOME PLEASURES: Socrates has shown us all this in order to demonstrate that many of the so-called pleasures are not pleasures at all. Many of the bodily "pleasures" are not true pleasures but are mere relief from pain. Satiety relieves hunger, but satiety is not in itself a pleasure, any more than is the absence of a headache, as we saw. Is it realistic, therefore, to pursue satiety as though it were a pleasure? What makes us think of this as a pleasure?

If we never know higher pleasures (+), we take the neutral states (0) as pleasurable. To a man who has always been in pain, the mere absence of it is bliss. But suppose we try to tell him that what he calls bliss is mere neutrality, and that there is yet a higher, positive pleasure. He cannot understand. We try to tell him that the opposite of black is white. And he insists that the opposite of black is grey.

The greatest satisfaction can come only from that which is most real. Knowledge has more unchanging reality than do things to eat or drink. As the body in the sensory world (B) is less real than is the soul which is in the intelligible world (A), so the pleasures of the body must be less real than the pleasures of the soul. Those who live entirely in the body have "pleasures" that go from minus to zero, from being hungry (-) to being fed (0). All their "pleasure"-seeking has pain mixed into it; it is all on the negative side of the scale.

The same is true of the spirited parts of the soul and their pleasures, when pursued without the use of reason. They, too, are unreal. It is reason alone that can impart some sort of reality to the pursuit of money or honor. So the best kind of pleasure (and the best kind of life) is one in which each faculty does its proper work and the whole thing is supervised by reason—as in the perfect state. In this alone is there happiness. But when the desire for money takes over and becomes ruler of all the rest, then happiness can only be illusory.

THE TYRANT'S PLEASURE IS UNNATURAL: The conclusion which we can draw from the foregoing is that the tyrant is at the farthest possible remove from natural, healthy pleasures, and the philosopher-king is the closest to these. To show how far apart they are, Socrates asks us to imagine that we have a continuum from the intellectual aristocracy of the philosopher-king to timocracy to oligarchy to democracy to tyranny. Thus, the pleasures of the tyrant are three steps removed from those of the oligarch—so that we might say that the tyrant's pleasures are one third those of the oligarch. Similarly, the pleasures of the oligarch are three steps removed from those of the philosopher-king, so that we might say that the oligarch's pleasures are one third those of the philosopher-king.

Accordingly, the pleasures of the philosopher-king are nine times as great as those of the tyrant. But this continuum is only a line. We must find a solid figure if we want to see the effect of this difference on life as a whole, "in the round." We must expand the line into a plane (9^2) and then raise the plane into a cube, and $9^3 = 729$. The tyrant has only $1/729$ of the happiness of the philosopher-king.

> **COMMENT:** This is all tongue-in-cheek, of course. Socrates would not be so foolish as to offer us a "hedonistic calculus" using numbers. This is *not*, therefore, intended as a serious proof by Socrates. Perhaps it is another parody of the Pythagoreans. It is very much their way of talking about such things as happiness. The mathematics of Plato and the Academy were of a far more significant order. Nowhere in Plato do we find anything like the Pythagorean technique of associating literal meanings with certain numbers. (Threes, nines, and their multiples always had a highly mystical meaning for the Pythagoreans. The number 729 must have been held to be a very powerful one. And Socrates tells us that it is nearly equal to the number of days and nights in a year of choices about pleasures and pains. Note that the emphasis, for Socrates, is always ethical.)

FRANKENSTEIN: Let us recall that Thrasymachus made the claim that the best kind of life, and the happiest, is to practice injustice and yet appear to be just. And let us recall that Socrates wants to demonstrate a psychological disproof of Thrasymachus' view. Socrates has, of course, given adequate justification for his view: not only by constructing a state but also in his powerful analyses of the various character-traits of unjust men. To top this off, he offers us a kind of allegory.

Let us construct a figure that will match the construction of the soul. It will be a figure made up of other figures. Corresponding to the desires, let us use a many-headed monster (who is able to grow another head as soon as we cut one off). Corresponding to the spirit, let us use the figure of a lion. And corresponding to reason, let us use the figure of a man. Let the first be the largest part, the third the smallest, and let the whole thing have the external shape of a man. Those who cannot look inside will see nothing but a man.

Now, is it a good thing to lead a life of injustice? What this entails is a life in which we feed the many-headed monster but starve the man in us. Then the man is weakened and is at the mercy of the monster and the lion, and these two will fight one another. But the best kind of life is one in which the man in us rules the rest. The man must care for the monster, letting certain heads grow but pruning others. He should make the lion his ally, and all should be in harmony. When a man cannot control the creatures within him he becomes their slave. And what profit is it to lead a life of injustice if it means enslavement? The highest purpose a man can have is that of preserving the health and harmony of his soul.

THE REPUBLIC, BOOK X

We are now in a position to appreciate the importance of the symbol of the Divided Line (Book VI, 509 D) for the entirety of Plato's thinking. He has used this symbol to illustrate his Theory of Forms and his Idea of the Good (Book VII). In Book IX, as we saw, he has used the significance of the Divided Line for the purpose of illustrating the unreality of many of the "pleasures." Here in Book X, he goes back to a concept he introduced early in Book III: the unreality of certain kinds of imitation, whether in art or politics. But he can now go further with this than he did in Book III. He can combine this theory with that of the Divided Line, and thereby make his condemnation of imitation even more powerful. All poetical imitations are injurious to our understanding. He admits his great love for Homer's poetry but he must reject it in favor of truth itself. (We can make this point immediate for ourselves by realizing that the Hollywood representation of God could be nothing like God as he really is. What Plato is condemning, in his condemnation of poetical imitation, is the view that would take MGM's God as literally true.)

IMITATION AND THE FORMS (596 A): When a number of things have a generic name in common, they also share an idea or form. When men create things, these things imitate these forms but are not the forms themselves. The carpenter makes individual beds (B1), but not the idea of a bed (A1). The poetic imitator can, of course, "make" everything. Like a mirror, he can reflect everything there is, but it is mere reflection (B2). He is a creator, but a creator of mere appearances. Artistic creation is therefore at the furthest remove from truth and reality!

The highest form of creation is God's creation of forms and concepts; next comes the human maker of things, imitating the forms; and last comes the artistic imitator. God makes only the *one* ideal form of each thing; the carpenter makes *many* imitations, none of them the "real" thing; the painter imitates only specific aspects of these particular things—you can look at his picture of a bed but you cannot sleep in it.

Plato is speaking in terms of symbols, of course, not strictly about beds and paintings. The question touches the entire relation of art to reality. How much does a playwright have to know about life in order to write a good play? Does Homer know that much? Plato asks, what state has ever been governed by the aid of Homer's writings? (599 D). Even the Sophists' doctrines have greater reality than do the poets'. We are in danger of being misled into thinking that artists have wisdom and can advise us. (On TV, they do this all the time. But why ought we to assume that if a man can act, he also knows something?)

CLASSIFICATION OF ARTS: There are those arts which use things, those which make things, and those which imitate them. The criterion of value, beauty and truth in art is the use to which the creation is put. The maker of a flute must conform to the demands of the user of the flute (the performer). The user has knowledge, therefore, and the maker will have opinion. But the imitator will have neither knowledge nor opinion, since he will be unable to say what it is that makes his work good or bad. Since it is not a kind of knowledge, imitation is nothing but a kind of play or sport.

Such arts play on our illusions (602 D). (There is op-art, for example. Also, there are *trompe l'oeil* paintings in which a painter can depict a doorway so marvelously that we are tempted to go through it.) But these illusions conflict with reality; our understanding tells us that such representations are not really what they represent. Since imitative art imitates things which do not have much reality to begin with (B1), we can therefore say of imitative art that it is an imitation of an imitation (B2). It is "an inferior who marries an inferior, and has inferior offspring" (603 B).

Nor is poetry any the more real. (That is why it is impossible to say whether a poem is true or false. It lives by imitation, by analogy. A proper piece of information, if it is true, almost *demands* the title of "truth" for itself. But poems and jokes are not information but insight; they can claim nothing; you see the point of them or you do not. "Explaining" them reduces them to something that is neither poem nor joke. Shelley might say, "Life, like a dome of many-colored glass, stains the white radiance of eternity." Shakespeare says the exact opposite in, "Life's but a walking shadow, a poor player," etc. Can we ask which of these two statements is correct? No, Plato would say, neither statement can be examined for its claim to truth or reality. If Plato were writing in the twentieth century, he would say that neither of these is a proper statement at all.)

One bad thing which poetry does is to get us to indulge in lamentation. This makes no sense, Plato feels. A healthy man will take stock of his situation soberly and will see what there is to be done. [There is a story which is the exact opposite to Plato's remarks about the man who loses his son (603 E). The story has it that the man was weeping, and a friend says, "Why do you weep? You cannot bring your son back by weeping." And the father answers, "That is why I weep."] For Plato, the lamentations of poetry do not appeal to the rational part of us but to the emotional part.

THE CRUX OF PLATO'S CRITICISM (605 B):   Poetry and painting imitate unreal objects; they are imitations of imitations. Further, they appeal to inferior parts of the soul. As we ought not to admit such influences into ourselves, lest they harm us by their unreality, neither ought we to admit such influences into our state. These evil influences may appear not so evil, or they may seem to be only potential evils, the kind against which we might be able to guard ourselves. But poetry has the power to produce actual harm in us. It teaches us to give in to sorrow and passion. And yet, when we are in actual misfortune, we naturally try to behave in a more restrained way; we do not behave as poetry bids us behave. Thus, poetry tries to unman us. How, then, can we admire poetry for this?

WHEN ART TRANSMITS EVIL: Does not the evil of others induce some measure of evil in ourselves? The sorrow of the characters in a tragic play becomes a sorrow of our own; the buffoonery we watch on the stage in a way makes buffoons of us. The same holds true for the other passions. How can we expect human beings to improve when art continually evokes the worst in them? No, although Homer is the greatest of poets, we cannot have him in our state. Let us have for our poetry only hymns to the gods and eulogies of famous men. If poets wish to operate in our state, let them defend their right to do so: let them show that their poetry is not only pleasant but useful. If poetry fails to do this, then we must reluctantly—like heartbroken lovers—give it up. The issue, Plato warns us, is an important one: whether a man is made good or bad (608 B). The condition of the soul in this short life is to be the basis of the soul's life hereafter.

IMMORTALITY: Glaucon is amazed that Socrates is willing to defend the idea of the soul's immortality. (There must have been considerable opposition to the idea on the part of Atomists such as Democritus.) Socrates says that there is no great difficulty in proving this. (In the *Phaedo*, we shall see that Socrates has a great deal of difficulty.)

Socrates' argument: All things have a good element that preserves them and an evil element that destroys them (as disease destroys the body, rust destroys iron, etc.) Certainly, it is not the good that will destroy a thing, so it must be the evil. If, therefore, anything has evil and is not destroyed by it, then nothing can destroy it. There is no question that the soul has its evils: unrighteousness, intemperance, cowardice, ignorance. But do these evils *destroy* the soul in the way that disease destroys the body? No. Do they separate the soul from the body? No. Then if the soul is not destroyed by the evils within it, it is hardly likely to be destroyed by a merely external force. Nor can we say that the soul is made evil by death, and that such an evil destroys the soul. If there is no vice in the soul that can kill it, then nothing can, and it lives forever.

THE PICTURE OF THE SOUL: If we want to see the soul in its true shape, we must look at it not as it is now, deformed by its contact with the body, encrusted with its ills. (It is one of Socrates' most cherished beliefs that bodily evils can effect psychological damage. The difference between body and soul is that when the body is injured, its wounds can heal. But with the soul this is extremely difficult if not impossible; the scars stay open.)

We must see the soul in its true shape, in its love of wisdom. (It is *this* that is natural to it, not injustice.) Thus, Socrates has claimed to vindicate the life of justice, not in terms of rewards but rather in terms of the effect of justice on the soul. Even if a man has absolute power and the ring of Gyges (Book II), it is still to his advantage, from a psychological point of view, to lead a life of justice.

REWARDS FOR JUSTICE (612 C):   To complete our picture, we ought to describe the rewards of a life of justice, even though this is definitely *not* part of his justification of it. It would weaken Socrates' point entirely if he were to say, "Be a just man because . . ." for in that case the whole point of justice would be overthrown as soon as the "because" were eliminated. We are just men not because there is a reward but because justice is the healthy way to operate. Nor is health a "because." It is merely the natural path. We do not say, "Be healthy, because. . . ."

The problem which Glaucon had set up in Book II was to weigh the life of justice against that of injustice and to put all the advantages on the side of injustice (to see whether a man would still be just even if there were no advantage in it). This imbalance must now be restored, Socrates says, because the value of justice in and for itself has been shown.

Which of these is more acceptable to the gods? And which kind of life are the gods likely to reward in *this* life? The unjust man appears to have the best of it at the outset, but this is not so in the long race. It is the just man who has the final gain. And so, the apparent advantages of the fortunate-but-unjust man must now be accorded to the just man, in addition to his advantage of having led the just life.

REWARDS FOR JUSTICE IN THE AFTER-LIFE (614 B):   The purpose of this section is not only to speak of rewards but also to give us a symbolic indication that justice is somehow part of the structure of the universe. This section is called The Myth of Er, a hero who was slain in battle and returned after death to tell about it. It is Socrates who repeats the story.

There were two openings in the earth, and two above them going into heaven. The judges sat in the space between. And after judgment, the just were directed to go to heaven by the opening on the right, and the unjust were told to go down into the opening on the left. Also, there were other paths, by which people came out of the earth all travel-worn, and others came back out of heaven all clean and bright. All these souls met in a meadow, and some recognized others, and each told what he had seen on his journey. Those underneath the earth had been there a thousand years. For any wrong they had done during earthly life, they had suffered ten times over during this thousand-year period. And the rewards of justice were ten-fold as well. Whenever any of them left the purgatory prematurely and tried to go into heaven, the opening would roar and they would be dragged back.

When the souls left the meadow, they came to a shaft of light extending from heaven into the earth. This column was brighter than a rainbow. The column is the axle of the universe. Here, Socrates describes the various spheres of the heavens, to which the planets and other bodies are attached. These make a harmony as they move. There are three Fates who sing in tune with this harmony. One sings of the past, one of the present, one of the future. As they sing, these daughters of Necessity touch the spheres to keep them moving.

> COMMENT: Socrates has already shown us that the reward-punishment system is part of the universal order. The cosmos is *not*—as it is for modern physics—a system that is value-neutral! Then he shows us that the "harmony" that is so vital to his philosophy is part of this universal order as well, and that the harmony is perfectly in tune with fate. Yet this is not a closed, deterministic system, as it is for modern physics. In order for values to exist, there must be freedom of choice—and Socrates must show this.

The travelling souls were offered new lives (617 D), on the condition that they must choose the quantity of virtue in their lives. They were allowed to choose lives that are long or short, tyrannical or just, famous or infamous, wealthy or poor, etc.

> COMMENT: The most important choice we can make is of this sort: there is no higher knowledge than that which enables us to discern good and evil. And all this can be based on nothing else but knowledge of one's soul. ("Know thyself.") How do we develop this knowledge of choices?

There was one soul who, in a former life, had been virtuous by habit. He could give no reasons for his actions; he had simply behaved virtuously. But he had no rational justification for virtue, so he lacked the ability to choose it. He therefore chose tyranny, and then discovered that he was destined, among other things, to eat his own children. He beat his breast and cried out and blamed his luck and the gods. The choice was his, however.

COMMENT: This is the view that is found also in Greek tragedy. The tragic hero thinks that his life was cruelly chosen by Fate—and so it is. But there is also that within him which justifies what the Fates have chosen. An Oedipus, without the destiny that the Fates marked out for him, would have done exactly what he did do. Greek Fate is not blind Fate. What is chosen for us is that which we really are. The thread of our lives is already spooled within us waiting to be spun out. The aim of Greek tragedy was to show that there is a harmony between Fate's decision and our own freedom. Socrates has exactly the same message, here. What the Fates have chosen is that which we freely choose.

By and large, the souls chose on the basis of what they knew in other lives. Those who had known no trials, no evil, now chose evil! Odysseus, after all his hardships, chose the quiet life of a private man. The three Fates *then* sealed the destinies chosen by the souls. The souls drank of the River of Forgetfulness. Those who were not wise, drank more than they had to (so that, in their new lives, they would find greater difficulty in getting wisdom—which is achieved by a kind of "recollection" of the eternal. See the *Meno*).

The next morning, they found themselves in earthly bodies, and they remembered nothing of how they got there.

GORGIAS

INTRODUCTION: The object of the *Republic* was to dramatize the concept of justice. Since the *Republic* is largely taken up with the views of Socrates, the opposing views of Thrasymachus and Glaucon are not given much of a defense. It might therefore be felt that the *Republic* does not really destroy the opposing views. Here in the *Gorgias*, however, the premise that force is the most fundamental political value is presented in a far more persuasive and sophisticated manner. The arguments of Callicles are harder to attack than were those of Thrasymachus. If that view is overthrown here then the victory of Socrates is greater than it was in the *Republic*.

The dialogue evolves in the following manner: (1) Socrates first talks to Gorgias, the famous teacher of oratory (an art that was of vital importance to the Athenian political system). This section asks whether oratory is an art at all. But this is only the introduction to a deeper issue. (2) In the interchange between Socrates and Polus, we see emerging the question of what is the highest value for mankind. (3) Finally, Socrates and Callicles have brought their opposing views to a climax, and we see an open conflict between two basic ways of looking at human existence.

Thus, the dialogue begins with a seemingly minor issue: whether oratory is an art. But the dialogue ends with a contrast of views—the life of wisdom *vs.* the pursuit of naked might. (It is such a contrast that leads us to ask ourselves about the role of power in our country's relations with the world. Unquestionably, our contemporary questions about global policy must finally come back to a philosophy of man.) The real theme of the dialogue is the justification of a way of life.

SOCRATES AND GORGIAS (449 D): What kind of art is it that Gorgias teaches? The most important of all, he says, since it prepares us for dealing with the most important concerns. This is the art with which we can persuade others to accept and support our views. Thus, this art gives us the instruments of power. (The question of what power is, and whether it is a good thing is the deeper question, but it will not be taken up until the third section.) The kind of persuasion that Gorgias teaches is the kind that can be used on crowds, and its subject matter is made up of issues of right and wrong. Socrates points out that we can persuade a crowd with or without instructing them. (When a politician addresses us, he can try to move us emotionally to his point of view without giving us any reasons for it.) For Gorgias, however, a successful orator need not be an "expert" in his subject. He does not need knowledge. He can convince a crowd better than an expert. But is this enough? Do we not need a knowledge of right and wrong?

Gorgias insists that he does not teach moral values, only the art of persuasion. If one of his students wants to use this skill for evil purposes, that is not the teacher's concern. (This is dangerous. It's the idea that knowledge is unrelated to values, and permits a scientist to develop the most deadly instruments for the most deadly purposes and then to claim that he is not responsible for the way his government uses them.) Since this is a skill that is used without knowledge, it follows that it is an art in which a man who knows nothing persuades people who know less. But oratory does involve issues of right and wrong, by Gorgias' own admission: we try to persuade someone that such-and-such is the right policy. How, then, can the student get these values if Gorgias admits that he does not teach them? Obviously, a deeper knowledge is needed.

SOCRATES AND POLUS (461 A): Socrates re-defines oratory as being not a kind of knowledge or art, but a talent or knack. (Jowett uses the word "experience" but that is a misleading translation.) Oratory is a talent for giving pleasure—like cooking. The cook pleases us; he does not care what the food might do to our system. Socrates shows that there are two true arts for the care of the body: one for maintaining the body in health (gymnastics) and one for restoring the sick body to health (doctoring). There are two true arts for the care of the soul: one for maintaining the soul in health (legislation: the art of making good laws) and another art for restoring a sick soul to health (justice: a judge's art of sentencing a criminal in order to rehabilitate him).

Each of these true arts has a corresponding counterfeit. Where gymnastics keeps us fit, adornment and padding merely make us look fit. Where doctoring restores us to health, cooking only pleases us. But in a competition between a doctor who prescribes a bitter medicine, and a cook who offers us a tasty dish instead, the cook wins only if the judges are children. Men know that they must choose the good over the pleasant. Similarly, where the true art of legislation keeps the soul of the state healthy, sophistry can sell us on any fad. And where true justice corrects ills, oratory persuades the crowd to take what is pleasant rather than what is good.

	True Arts	*False Arts*
Maintaining body	Gymnastics	Adornment
Restoring body	Doctoring	Cooking
Maintaining soul	Legislation	Sophistry
Restoring soul	Justice	Oratory

Polus says that oratory is not counterfeit since the orator's power is tremendous and real. Shouldn't we admire a man who has been able so effectively to sway a crowd that he can have absolute power and can kill anybody? (Think of Hitler.) Socrates says that such a man is rather to be pitied than admired. To commit an act of injustice is worse for the soul than to be the victim of injustice. The question therefore comes down to the one discussed in the *Republic*: who is the happier man, the evil or the just one? Polus says that the evil man is even happier if he is not punished. But Socrates demonstrates that the tyrant who lives a life of injustice and is too powerful to be punished is like a sick man who will not see a doctor. Such a man must be *less* happy if he is not punished, since the evil in him is not corrected. If smooth talk enables the orator to "get away with murder," then it is himself he is injuring with his oratory; he denies himself a cure.

SOCRATES AND CALLICLES (418 C): Callicles presents the most powerful and extended argument of the three. He raises the level of the discussion by showing us the political implications. And with his entrance into the discussion, the dialogue suddenly glows with realism. He is no mere theoretician like Gorgias and Polus; he is a man involved in political life. When Callicles defends the negative view, we have the feeling that there is a good deal of genuine experience behind it.

He sees it as a law of nature (and of politics) that the strong do what they will, and the weak suffer what they must. Force is the only reality. It is natural for a strong man to trample the conventions which the society of the weak have erected in order to protect themselves against the strong. Sufficient might makes right. (He is against the morality of the weak, not against morality as such. The strong man makes his own morality, and his strength is its justification.) This is a law of nature, and as such it is superior to mere conventions. We must not set up conventional injunctions against the conqueror—since he is merely acting in accordance with nature.

Socrates points out that if justice is whatever the stronger says it is, then society is stronger than the individual and therefore its conventions must be superior—by the very same principle with which Callicles condemned them! Callicles explains that he does not mean physical strength, merely, when he speaks of the stronger. The superior man is one who is better and wiser.

The law of nature is that such pre-eminent individuals should rule.

It is natural for a man to have desires and to fulfill them, Callicles says. The freedom to get what we want and to do what we please—this is what is natural in us, and this is what makes a happy life. But this concept of immediate gratification of all impulses leads Callicles into difficulties. If his view is correct, there is no place for the separation of good from bad impulses, for all of them must be satisfied. And yet he tries to make just such a distinction. Where does this conflict lead?

It leads to the point where the decision as to which life is the *best* one—the pursuit of wisdom or the pursuit of power over multitudes—cannot be decided on this rejected basis of pleasure and pain. How can we say which life is *best*, if "best" is not a term we may use (that is, if terms such as "good" and "bad," "best" and "worst" must be rejected because *all* pleasures are to be pursued)? This means that if Callicles insists that it is natural for men to satisfy *all* desires, he cannot say that the pursuit of power is the best of those desires. To say that one is best is to say that some are inferior, and this would imply that not all should be satisfied.

Any attempt, therefore, to slur over the distinction between good and bad (which is what Callicles must do) is fatal to the judgment as to which is the good life. But to practice *any* art properly—whether ice-skating or crowd-swaying—we must know which are the right and the wrong procedures. So we need value-terms from the start, we need standards. A false art, such as oratory, has no standards but that of the public it seeks to flatter. What we need, for all human problems, however, is the use of intelligence. And this already indicates the kind of life that is best and most natural. Socrates speaks of himself as the only true statesman of his time since he is the physician of the state, caring for its good—not its pastry-chef, caring for its pleasures. For this work of his, Socrates ominously predicts that he may someday be put to death by the very people he has benefited!

MENO

INTRODUCTION: This dialogue continues with the issues presented in the *Gorgias*, and also prepares us for the more complex theories of the *Protagoras* and the *Phaedo*. Let us recall that Gorgias admitted that he could not teach a man how to be good. (We will see the issue again taken up in the *Protagoras*.) The question of whether virtue can be taught is first taken up here in the *Meno*.

> **COMMENT:** The word for "virtue," or "goodness" is *arete* in Greek. This is not the Victorian idea of virtue: chastity in a woman. Nor does it mean the Roman "virtus," which is courage and manliness. What *arete* means is an ability—the ability to lead a life in which we fulfill ourselves and do all things that are part of being a man. A Rhodes scholar (brilliant in studies, excelling in sports, prominent in student government) would be a perfect example of *arete*. Can this be taught? Are such talents born or made?

Meno asks, at the outset: Can *arete* be taught? Or is it acquired by practice? Or is it something inborn? Socrates suggests that we must first define what this "goodness," this "virtue," is. Gorgias had said that there are different kinds of "virtues" or "abilities" appropriate to different kinds of people: the ability proper to a man is to be a success in public life; the ability proper to a woman is to be a good homemaker. Young and old, slave and free—even strong man and weak man—each has his special virtue, according to Gorgias.

What Socrates wants, however, is not this enumeration of examples. (If you are asked for a definition of a horse, it makes little sense to answer, "There are white ones, black, brown, spotted, palomino, etc.") What Socrates wants is the *definition* of goodness—that which all the examples of goodness have in common. There must be one kind of "good" that is basic to them all, and therefore Gorgias is wrong in saying that there are different "goodnesses" for different people.

MENO'S DEFINITION OF GOODNESS (77 A): "Goodness is the desire of things that are honorable, and the power to get them." Socrates has two criticisms of this definition. First, the definition seems to say that a man could *knowingly* desire that which is evil. (In the *Protagoras*, he will show that this is not possible.) Men might desire an evil thing if they mistakenly think it is good. But for a man to desire something means that he holds it to be "desirable"—that is, "good." So the qualification of "honorable" is not needed. Meno's definition is thereby reduced to "goodness is the desire of things and the power to get them"—or, "goodness is the power to get the things that are desired (as being good)"—or, "goodness is the power to get good things" (things such as wealth, health, respect, etc.).

But does "power to get" include any evil means? No, for then it is no longer good. So we have to add that "goodness is the power to get good things by using good means." But if we add this qualification (as we must), then we are using the term "good" in order to explain "good"—which is circular reasoning. (This is Socrates' second objection to Meno's definition: if we draw out the definition to its implications, it destroys itself.) We must inquire again.

MENO'S PARADOX (80 D): Meno contends that we cannot inquire about anything. If you already know it, there is no need to inquire. And if you do not know it, you would not recognize the answer when you encounter it. How, then, is it possible to learn anything? Speaking in metaphor, Socrates answers by saying that the soul is immortal, and that before it entered its earthly body, the soul understood all things. Now it has forgotten these things and it must struggle to remember them. (Whenever we know a deep truth, it is like knowing something that is part of us, something remembered from another life.) Thus, real learning is nothing but a "recollection," and inquiry is *not* impossible. Learning is not a passive taking in of information. It is an active struggle to "recollect" —a striving to "get at" the truth.

SOCRATES AND THE SLAVE (82 A): To illustrate the idea of "recollection," Socrates questions Meno's slave boy who never studied mathematics. Socrates draws a square with a diagonal. Let us say the square is two by two feet, or four feet square. Now, Socrates asks the boy, if we wanted to draw a figure twice as large as this (eight feet square) how long should the sides be? Since the sides of the original square are two feet, the sides of the new square should be four feet, the boy says. But Socrates shows him that this would give us a square that is sixteen feet square, not eight feet square. The boy tries another answer and is shown to be wrong again. Socrates points out that this is real progress: at least the boy knows, now, that he does not know.

Socrates gets him to draw the answer. We may simplify this in the following way: by drawing a new square from the diagonal of the old one, we get a square that is twice the area. The old

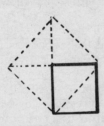

square is made of two equal triangles. The new square is made up of four of the same triangles. Thus, the new square is twice the area of the old. If S stands for the side of the original square, and d stands for its diagonal, then we may say that although S and d are incommensurable, yet their relation can be expressed as $d^2 = 2S^2$. The actual diagram which Socrates draws is

more elaborate and goes like this:

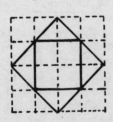

Let the heavy line describe our original square of two by two, or four square feet. The dashed line represents the boy's first suggestion to double the length. But this gives us a square that is four times as large, not twice as large. The thin solid line, however, represents a figure of exactly eight square feet, since it contains the original four square feet as well as eight triangles of one-half a square foot each. Thus, four plus four gives us eight square feet!

The point is that the boy knew none of this at the start. And Socrates gave him no "information." The boy must have got this knowledge from within himself, "recollecting" it—or recollecting what he *knew* but had forgotten. If he had this knowledge in him, and did not get it during his lifetime, he must have got it "before he was born." (This idea will be found again in the *Phaedo*.)

SOCRATES' RE-DEFINITION OF VIRTUE (87 B): Only if virtue is knowledge, can it be taught. Only knowledge can be "recollected." In the *Protagoras*, Plato will show that all virtues are kinds of knowledge. This means that we can call our acts virtuous only if we can establish them on rational principles—that is, if we know what we are doing. The act that is proper but done unconsciously from habit is not really good, therefore. Intelligence is what is required to make an act good. The so-called "goods"—wealth, health, respect—can all be turned into evils if pursued without thought. Thus, virtue and knowledge are necessarily part of one another.

PROTAGORAS

INTRODUCTION: The question, can virtue be taught? has many profound implications: Can we have a science of values? Is a science of man possible? Unless we can find a *principle* underlying man's behavior we cannot have a science. Similarly, unless we can find a principle and underlying all virtue, *it* cannot be taught. The implications come to this: our answer to the question can virtue be taught? will determine whether a science of man is possible, and whether education is a science.

We can appreciate this in connection with the universal situation of raising children. Are children really "raised" by some rational means available to us as "raisers"? Or do children "grow" by some mysterious internal process susceptible to no external control? Is humanness something which the child absorbs automatically in a thousand trivial moments of trial and reinforcement? Can that which we sum up as "character" or "personality" be taught at all? Socrates' answer is the one for which he has prepared us in the *Meno*: the only thing that can be taught is that which can be articulated in words and principles. Teaching someone how to play golf is not "teaching" but showing how. And, as we saw in the *Meno*, learning cannot take place in a passive relation in which one "gives" learning and the other "takes."

THE PLAN OF THE DIALOGUE: Protagoras begins by maintaining that virtue *can* be taught (he is a professional teacher, after all). Socrates holds that virtue *cannot* be taught. By the time the dialogue ends, the two men have apparently reversed their positions. Protagoras now says that virtue cannot be taught. Socrates now says that virtue can be taught. This is not, however, a genuine reversal of position. Socrates has merely re-defined what we are to mean by virtue. His position was consistent from beginning to end: if what we mean by virtue is the conventional morality of society, then this is not taught. But

virtue is something entirely different from conventional morality. Virtue is knowledge, and in this sense alone can we say
that virtue can be taught.

Besides being one of the masterpieces of Plato's dramatic technique, this dialogue is also the one in which Socrates'
differences with the Sophists are stated most completely. What
it does is to probe down to the assumptions that underlie all
Sophistic thinking: the Relativism which says that men (not
Man) are the measure of all things, and that values vary with
their cultural milieu. Socrates, it will be recalled, takes a stand
that is in complete contrast to this: he is an Absolutist who
says that the Truth is the measure of all things; there is one
Truth, although there are many opinions about it.

THE DIALOGUE OPENS: Here there is an interesting piece of
stage-business: Socrates is awakened before dawn by Hippocrates, who relates the news that the great Protagoras is in
town. Hippocrates is eager to study under the famous professor
and wants Socrates to introduce him. Since it is too early to go
to him, they spend the time talking about Sophists and what it
is that they teach. Socrates is aware that, in real learning, the
soul is changed. It is important to know, therefore, exactly
what one may expect to receive from Protagoras, so we may
know whether the soul is to be changed for good or ill. And
what is it, actually, that Protagoras teaches? The Sophist is like
an importer of foreign delicacies (compare the *Gorgias*, where
the Sophist is spoken of as a kind of pastry-cook). Before one
takes these intellectual tidbits into one's system, one ought to
consult a physician—a "physician of the soul"—for advice.

When they finally meet Protagoras, Socrates (speaking as the
"physician" of Hippocrates) asks the great celebrity what
advantages a student might expect to receive by studying under
him. The answer is that he will improve daily. Improve in
what? He will gain prudence in affairs public and private. He
will know how to manage his "house" better and how to speak
in the best interests of the state.

> **COMMENT:**   We ought next to ask: How are we to rec-
> ognize the state's best interest? Does not this require a
> knowledge of a deeper kind? The question is not raised
> here, since it is the point of the dialogue as whole, and
> Plato wants to get to that point in a natural manner.

What Socrates does ask is whether this skill is at all capable of being taught. Can we produce great men by teaching? Can we *teach* statesmanship? (If so, then it ought to be possible to *produce* an infinite number of Jeffersons and Monroes.)

ATHENIAN BELIEF: Socrates says that it is an implicit part of the Athenian way of life to hold that statesmanship cannot be taught: in any sort of question requiring an expert's opinion, we call an expert. But in matters of state, we listen to everybody's opinion regardless of his qualifications. It would seem, then, that the Athenians feel that statesmanship (or virtue, or goodness) is *not* the sort of thing that can be taught or can be acquired by study. The great statesmen cannot teach it to their sons, obviously, because no one can teach it. Protagoras answers with a myth.

PROTAGORAS' MYTH OF SOCIAL EDUCATION (320 C): When men and animals were being created, Epimetheus was assigned to distribute among them certain qualities, skills and gifts. The animals were fully equipped before it was realized that all the gifts had been given out and that there was nothing left for man. (What man can build as efficiently as a sparrow or as a spider?) Man would be utterly helpless—without fur, a tail, hooves, claws or wings. To make up for these disadvantages, Prometheus stole from heaven the various crafts and fire and gave these gifts to man. Now men were somewhat better off. But they did not have the social arts. So Zeus sent his messenger to distribute among men a sense of justice and righteousness. These were not to be distributed only to a few, the way the skills are. No, the sense of justice and righteousness had to be given to everyone in the same measure.

> **COMMENT:** What Protagoras is maintaining is the familiar view that men's values arise in their struggle with nature. The social structure, also, is the outgrowth of this struggle. Their social nature is an instinct implanted equally in all men so we ought not to be surprised that all men are listened to in Athens. Socrates would answer to this: it is all very well to speak of instincts. But the only time a man ought to be listened to is when he *knows*. There is a vast gulf between instinct and knowledge.

PROTAGORAS' POSITION: Protagoras maintains that social values can be taught. When we punish someone, it is in an effort to teach him. We do not punish someone for what he cannot help, but only when there is a condition to be corrected by learning. Even though there is an instinctual social nature in all men, it is something that must be developed in us by our contacts with culture as a whole. All our lives are spent in learning the values which our society "teaches" us. Protagoras describes at length the way in which we are being taught at every moment of our lives—from the time we are in the care of nursemaids up through the time when the law is our teacher. Thus, everyone learns the virtues. And the sons of politicians are not exposed to more of these influences than is anyone else. Protagoras merely claims that he is better able than most others to teach virtue.

> **COMMENT:** For Protagoras, virtues are determined by society and are relative to it. For Socrates, however, true virtue is a matter of rational principles and these cannot be merely relative—any more than mathematics can be relative.

ARE ALL THE VIRTUES ONE? (329 C): No, Protagoras says. The various social qualities are all parts of virtue, but they differ from one another—as the parts of a face are different, yet are part of one face. For it is clear to Protagoras that a man might be brave and unjust, or just yet unwise. The virtues are different from each other, and each has its own function. But would it not follow, Socrates points out, that if justice and piety (holiness) are not the same, then we can have an unholy justice? Could justice be unholy? Could holiness be unjust? Protagoras retracts somewhat, and says that there possibly is a relation between justice and holiness, but what that relation is he cannot say. Socrates says that each thing has only one opposite. Agreed. Then if wisdom is the opposite of foolishness, and if temperance also is the opposite of foolishness, it follows that wisdom and temperance must be the same, or that temperance is a kind of wisdom. Yet Protagoras had said that they are different.

Thus, we have seen how justice and holiness are the same, and how wisdom and temperance are the same. Now, we ought to be able to bring together justice-holiness with wisdom-temperance. Can a man be unjust, yet temperate? (333 B). In other words, is it possible to say that injustice is "good sense"? Protagoras, speaking as a Relativist, says that the good of something is relative to the user: hay is good for horses, not for man, and so on. Socrates finds fault with the lengthiness of Protagoras' remarks, and the discussion is about to break up. The two antagonists are finally persuaded by the audience to continue the discussion. Protagoras wants to shift the discussion onto the topic of poetry.

THE POEM OF SIMONIDES: There is a tedious analysis that appears to have little relation to the subject-matter of the discussion. Some scholars have seen in this nothing more than a bit of humorous relief (as when Socrates says that the Lacedaemonians—the Spartans, who are distinguished for not having produced one thinker, poet or statesman—really are wise men but have managed to keep it a secret). There is, however, a serious point to be made here. The Sophists claimed as one of their skills the art of interpreting poetry so as to squeeze the literal meaning from it. Our discussion shows that in two conflicting poetic statements, neither statement can be said to be "true." We saw this in the *Republic*. Poetry does not state its insights in a rational manner—any more than do proverbs and conventional wisdom. Suppose I see someone suffering, and I say to him, "Every cloud has a silver lining," and someone else says, "Into each life, a little rain must fall." Which of these is correct? Protagoras assumes that it is possible to say which line of poetry is correct and which is incorrect. The analysis of the poem of Simonides shows how far from wisdom poetry really is.

The poem champions a kind of moral mediocrity, ending with praise for the man who does no evil voluntarily (as though involuntary evil is all right). The reason why this is mediocre is that it makes it easy to hide behind ignorance and so avoid moral responsibility. What Simonides' poem is saying is that if we do evil "involuntarily" it is not as bad as doing it voluntarily.

Socrates attacks this by showing that no man does evil involuntarily or unknowingly. If I say, "I know this is wrong but I can't help myself," then I really do *not* know it to be wrong. The test of knowing and believing is action. In this way, Socrates identifies virtue with reason. I might be mistaken as to what is good or evil. But if I do an evil, it is because I temporarily think it a good thing. Sin is ignorance, as virtue is knowledge.

THE DISCUSSION RESUMES (349 A): Are wisdom, temperance, courage, justice and holiness five names for the same thing, or are they essentially different? Protagoras says that there is a considerable similarity between them, except for courage which is quite different. A man can be brave and ignorant. (This is to be the test, then. If courage, too, can be shown to be a kind of knowledge, then all the rest of the virtues are knowledge as well.)

Socrates shows that true confidence comes only with knowledge, when we *know* what we are doing. Unknowing confidence is mere recklessness. But Protagoras refuses to identify courage with confidence. The courageous are confident, but not all the confident are courageous. "Confidence" may be due to madness, but courage is part of a man's nature. (In other words, neither of these have to do with knowledge.) To answer this, Socrates takes a roundabout path.

GOOD AND EVIL AS PLEASURE AND PAIN: Socrates takes the view most opposed to his own—in order to refute it. It must be emphasized to the reader that Socrates is not adopting Hedonism—the theory whereby *all* good and evil are nothing but pleasure and pain. His motive in temporarily taking this stand is to show that if even this most anti-intellectual way of life depends on intelligence for its most efficient functioning, then *all* virtue is knowledge. If there is no theory of behavior that can ignore the role of intelligence, then all value rests on knowledge.

Socrates combines this idea with the point he made earlier that no man does evil knowingly. Can we be led to behave against our "better judgments"? No, the best judgment we can make is the way we do behave. If good and evil are reduced to pleasure and pain, then it is absurd to say that a man is overcome by pleasure and that pleasure makes him do what he would rather not do. He cannot say (if everything is pleasure or pain) that he would prefer not to overeat. If overeating gives him pleasure then he has no reason—according to his own theory—for not overeating. If he fears that his overeating will give him a future pain, then pleasure and pain are still the criteria of action. And if this is so, then the great life-principle becomes the art of measuring—that is, pleasure must be reduced to a science. Even here, then, in this most lowly of life-standards, intelligence is the cornerstone of successful operation.

The only thing by which a man can be overcome is ignorance. Whatever he does he actually believes to be good. No man does an evil act if he knows another act is better and attainable. No man knowingly does evil; he may say that it is evil, but he does it because he thinks it is good. To prefer evil to good is not in human nature.

A man, therefore, cannot be couragous and ignorant since *all* virtues are identical with knowledge. For a man to be courageous *and* ignorant, it would be necessary for him to have knowledge, *and* not to know.

CONCLUSION: Socrates began by saying that virtue could not be taught. But now he says that it *can* be taught, provided that all virtue is knowledge. Only knowledge can be taught. Protagoras began by saying that virtue could be taught. But now he is eager to show that virtue is anything but knowledge, and is therefore incapable of being taught.

THEAETETUS

INTRODUCTION: The casual reader may think that Plato is himself being casual—since he rarely comes to a conclusion. But that is the point of the dialogues, precisely, and it is by no means a casual point: each inquiry must lead to further questioning. There can be no conclusion to this (in the sense of a completion). For this reason, it is always possible to find some continuity between one dialogue and another—as in the case of *Protagoras* and the present dialogue. The *Protagoras* is an early dialogue, and it ends with the apparent "conclusion" that virtue is knowledge. But this is no conclusion (in the sense of a completion to all inquiry) since we can still ask, "What is knowledge?" It is in this late dialogue, the *Theaetetus*—written at least twenty years after the *Protagoras*—that the question (What is knowledge?) is taken up. There will be three attempts at an answer, and each will be shown to be inadequate. Demonstrating their inadequacy has the greatest significance because it can make clear the way to further clarification and definition. Negative knowledge is of great value. If we were looking for the cause of cancer, it would save us a lot of trouble if we could rule out certain possibilities at the start.

KNOWLEDGE IS PERCEPTION (151 E): This version of "seeing is believing" is the first definition offered by Theaetetus. Socrates immediately relates this idea to the famous statement of Protagoras: man is the measure of all things. (Here is another instance of the continuity between the two dialogues.) According to Socrates' interpretation, Protagoras meant his statement to apply to individuals: Men are the measure of all things—for themselves. In the view of Protagoras, there would be no such entity as the abstract "man," in the absolute. There are only men, and it is they who are the judges of what is hot or cold, pleasant or unpleasant. All perceived qualities are personal in nature. None of them refer to an objective reality which we can all perceive in the same way. If A says the wind is cold, it *is* cold for him. And if B says the wind is warm, it *is* warm for him. The wind itself, taken objectively, cannot be said to be cold or warm apart from its being perceived as cold or warm by someone. Qualities (such as warmth or color) are neither *in* the object nor *in* the perceiver, but occur when the two come into contact (153 E). (This is not subjectivism. A subjectivist would say that qualities are *only* in the mind. Protagoras does not say this. Qualities are in the contact of mind and world.)

The way that men judge things to be, that is the way things really are. Protagoras does not imply that our reports are mere opinions or subjective fancies. When A says the wind is cold, it *is*. A's report is "incorrigible" (uncorrectable)—that is, there is no outside reality by which we can correct A's report in favor of B's. A is absolutely correct, and there is no way of contradicting him. Suppose we show him a thermometer that reads 85°F, and we say that this means that the wind is warm, he could admit that such a reading has always indicated warmth to him, but that now the wind is cold to him. (He might be ill.) His position can in no way be shaken. As long as we assume that no sense-description reports things objectively, then there can be no conflict between the reports of A and B. This theory of the "incorrigibility" of sense-data has received great attention in recent years. (See A. J. Ayer, *The Foundations of Empirical Knowledge*.) Socrates overthrows the theory.

CRITICISMS OF THIS THEORY (161 A): From the theory, it would follow that any being with senses—even an animal—is made the "measure of all things." Further, if each man is the measure of his own "reality," then how can Protagoras rank his own knowledge over the knowledge of those whom he teaches? Furthermore, if knowledge were the same as perception, the mere act of hearing a foreign language should be equivalent to understanding it. But this is not so. I can *perceive* a foreigner's words without *knowing* what he says. Further, if knowledge were the same as perception, then as soon as I cease to perceive I should cease to know. Yet I can shut my eyes and remember something, and know it, when I no longer perceive it.

As to there being no "objective reality" outside us, we must point out that men do use the words "true" and "false," purporting to describe reality objectively (170 D). When they use these words, they imply that things really are so or so—and that it is not merely their own experience that they are talking about. This means that when A and B give conflicting reports, they cannot both be "incorrigible," but one report must be false if the other is true. Further, if all reports were "incorrigible," there could be no "right" or "wrong." We know, however, that people can regard an action as being right, and yet be completely wrong about it. This implies that there *is* an objective reality out there, and that *it* makes our reports right or wrong —that is, an objective reality of which men are not the measure.

KNOWLEDGE IS TRUE OPINION (187 B):   We have to insert the word "true," because knowledge is not equivalent to opinion, *per se*, since there can be true as well as false opinions. Can we say, then, that knowledge is true opinion? Now, an opinion can be true without involving knowledge. A primitive person could have the true opinion that the bark of a certain tree is a good cure for a certain disease, but he might have false knowledge of why this is so; he might say that the bark cures the disease because the tree belongs to a certain god.

What is it to have a false opinion? Let us compare the mind to an aviary, a cage filled with birds. In a certain sense, we do "have" the birds. But being able to put one's hand on precisely the bird that is needed is quite another thing. Thus, we may possess certain knowledge, yet be unable to put our hands on it at the right time—as anyone knows who has ever taken a difficult exam.

Another example of true opinion that does not involve knowledge is this (see 201 C): Suppose that a man is on trial for murder. He is really guilty but the evidence against him is slight. The prosecutor manipulates the evidence and appeals to the emotions of the jurors, so that the jury is led to vote "guilty." This happens to be a correct opinion on their part (because the man really is guilty) but their opinion was not based on knowledge (since they made their verdict on the basis of manipulated evidence and their emotions).

KNOWLEDGE IS TRUE OPINION PLUS EXPLANATION (201 D): Theaetetus attempts to correct the weaknesses of the second definition by adding the condition of an explanation. But what is this? In scientific explanation, we attempt to get down to the simplest elements. Let us say we reduce all knowledge to its most fundamental "atomic" constituents. But that does not mean that we can explain the complexity, for we can spell out a word letter by letter, without knowing what it means.

Is the complex reducible to an enumeration of the elements? We can say that a car is made of four wheels, a transmission, a carburetor, six cylinders, an oil filter, etc. But suppose we have all these things sent to us in a box. We still would not have a car. Knowledge, therefore, is not a matter of reducing things to their elements, but rather of putting them together so as to form the complex reality. (Such eminent thinkers as Hume, Marx and Freud all commit the intellectual sin of "reductionism," whereby they make statements that read: "Man is *nothing but* a . . ." If scientific theory is nothing but reduction then one is tempted to say, with Goethe, *"Grau ist all' Theorie. . . ."*) (All theory is gray.)

Thus, three definitions of knowledge have been proposed, and all three have been rejected. The rejections are, however, of the highest importance. To know, for example, that knowledge is not sensation is already a tremendous step forward. The true definition of knowledge would have to combine criteria of truth with criteria of reality. This is done in the Divided Line, the *Republic*, Book VI.

PHAEDRUS

INTRODUCTION: The *Phaedrus* and the *Symposium* are the "mystic" dialogues. It might surprise us that a superbly rational and realistic thinker such as Socrates can have in him as well the qualities of a visionary. Socrates is able to combine into a unity subjects that appear to have the widest diversity. Here in the *Phaedrus*, there is a discussion about literary style that is at the same time a discussion about erotic love! But we shall see how (here and in the *Symposium*) he takes the subject of love onto a new level altogether, so that it serves as an allegorical representation of the mystic quest.

THE ESSAY OF LYSIAS: The dialogue opens with a discussion of an essay by Lysias, a teacher of literary style. It would be the object of such a technician to show that he could convince you of the value of an idea you would normally reject. If this master of style could make you agree that Jack-the-Ripper was really a gentle soul, then he could "prove" anything. The aim, then, is to get the "sickest" possible idea and prove its cogency —thereby demonstrating the high skill of the writer. This is what Lysias does with the concept of love.

Homosexuality was practiced extensively in the Greek world. It was believed, however, that this way of life could be justified by the sincerity and nobility of the feelings involved. But Lysias "proves" the opposite, namely that calculation is better than sincerity (in other words, that prostitution is smarter than honest passion because prostitution "pays off"). The essay lists the supposed advantages of cold calculation as against the uncertainties of "love." The "cold" relationship is one in which both parties quietly get what they want; the "passionate" relationship is beset with quarrels, jealousies, etc.

SOCRATES' FIRST VIEW (237 A): Phaedrus challenges Socrates to compose a better essay on the madness of love. Of course, Socrates is not going to do this as a display of depraved values, nor as an exercise in persuasion for its own sake. He is much too serious about the content of his composition to treat it in such cavalier fashion. The elementary distinction he makes is one which we saw in the *Gorgias* and in the *Republic*. It is a highly moralistic distinction which, if ignored, can corrupt governments as easily as individuals: the distinction between *pleasant* and *good*.

Love, Socrates says, is a desire which is one of two kinds: either the inborn desire for the pleasant or the acquired desire for the good. When reason wins out, the good is chosen over the merely pleasant, and temperance reigns. When the appetites win out, the choice is for the pleasant, and then passion (or excess) reigns. There are many forms of passion, and love is one of these. Socrates defines it as "intense desire aroused by beauty and in conflict with reason" (238 C).

When Socrates condemns passion it is not because he favors cold calculation; rather, it is because passion conflicts with reason. Thus, the discussion is immediately raised to a higher ethical level. The disadvantage of the passionate relationship is that it enslaves the beloved, prevents him from having a mind of his own, or from exercising his reason freely. Here, it is not mere jealousy that is condemned (as in Lysias' essay) but the sort of jealousy on the part of the lover that prevents the beloved from fulfilling all his potentialities. The ills of the passionate relationship make a long list. (We need only think of the possessive and sado-masochistic aspects of some heterosexual love-relationships.)

Socrates has been saying all this with his face covered, because he is ashamed of his words. They could be taken as an offense against the god Eros. Socrates will not go into the supposed advantages of the non-lover. It is enough to say that he has all the advantages which the lover lacks. Socrates would prefer to say no more, but he hears from his "divine sign," which always forbids. He feels guilty of impiety to the great god, and so he must make the proper atonement. He will state his real views on love.

SOCRATES' SECOND VIEW (244 A):   Socrates had described passion as a kind of madness. But there are four forms of madness which are god-sent and good: (1) prophecy, in the way the prophets are "possessed" by the god and speak in a kind of ecstasy; (2) the ritual inspiration that can purge away guilt;

(3) poetry, another form of divine madness in which the gods rob us of part of our minds so that we may utter *their* mind (see the *Ion*, 534 C); (4) love, another form of "inspiration" (literally, a state in which a spirit has been "breathed into" us).

This takes Socrates into an allegorical description of the soul. It is a charioteer with a pair of winged steeds. (The charioteer is reason, the steeds are the higher "spirit" and the lowlier "appetites." See the diagram, above, in the *Republic*, Book IV.) Thus, the soul circles heaven in its chariot. But the two horses, being so different, are difficult to manage. For some charioteers, the horses respond to the slightest suggestion of the whip. For others, the horses are unruly. They lose their wings and then the soul falls to earth, entering an earthly body which it carries around like a living tomb. Those whose horses have been most obedient to control enter into the bodies of men of orderly nature: philosophers and lovers of beauty. There is a graded series all the way down to the most disorderly types: sophists, demagogues, tyrants.

The soul must grow new wings before it can return to the heavens, but this takes ten thousand years. For the philosopher or the philosophic-lover, however, the period is only three thousand years if this soul chooses the philosopher's life three times in three successive incarnations. (See the Myth of Er, *Republic*, Book X.)

The wings are made to grow by means of our ability to "recollect" (see the *Meno*) the things which the soul saw in heaven. What we see in experience reminds us only dimly. But the sight of earthly beauty stirs our recollection of something divine. Our wings begin to grow. This is what real love can do for us— develop us spiritually—whereas a "cold" relationship is a distortion of spirit.

With this, Socrates can now attack at length the question of what constitutes good writing: it is knowledge of the truth, not the power to convince us that a falsehood is true—as Lysias had attempted to do. It is in the light of the truth, alone, that the integration of the soul can take place. Accordingly, Socrates ends the dialogue with a prayer: "Beloved Pan, and all ye other gods who haunt this place, give me beauty in the inward soul; and may the outward and the inward be at one. . . ."

SYMPOSIUM

INTRODUCTION: This dialogue is rivalled only by the *Protagoras* for dramatic perfection. In addition, there are subtle touches of insight, as well as expository writing of the highest order. But above all, there is the way in which a moment of supreme mystic elevation (which, in essence, *cannot* be put into words) is presented to us in dramatic form.

The scene is a dinner party to celebrate Agathon's winning the dramatic prize for his first tragedy. The characters are Phaedrus, Pausanias, Eryximachus, Aristophanes, Agathon and Socrates. Each will take his turn speaking, and finally Alcibiades will descend on the party like a *deus ex machina*. The theme of the discussion is love. The talk begins on the lowest physical level, rises gradually to the technical, the allegorical and then the spiritual level—only to be surpassed by the mystical. Thus, we find in the dialogue the same dialectical process (of broadening and deepening the question) that we might expect if this were a conversation between Socrates and one other person.

Before the dinner begins, we are told that Socrates is in a doorway, standing like a statue. He is in one of his mystic "transports" and is oblivious to all words. For the reader, this plants the seeds of the expectation of something in a high mystic order. It is what we might call a "narrative hook."

PHAEDRUS (178 A): Phaedrus speaks of love in the sense of the physical homosexual relationship. (As we saw in the previous dialogue, the *Phaedrus*, this is the sort of thing that Socrates frowns upon.) Since Phaedrus (the same character as in the other dialogue) is an admirer of literary style, we can expect of him precisely the contribution he makes, praising Eros for being the oldest of deities, and so on. He also praises Eros for bestowing the greatest of benefits on man: when homosexual lovers are soldiers they fight more bravely, for fear of disgracing themselves in the eyes of their beloved. (This passage, trivial as it is, speaks volumes about what such a man regards as the greatest of the benefits which the god has bestowed on man.)

PAUSANIAS (180 C): Pausanias makes a distinction which Socrates would inevitably have made at this point (had this been a conversation between Socrates and one other person). It is the habit of Socrates to draw a moral distinction from everything. There are good and bad loves, Pausanias says, a heavenly and a "common" or earthly. The earthly love is characterized by the fact that it is generally heterosexual and physical.

> **COMMENT:** The reason for his low estimate of heterosexual relationships can be explained by the fact that Athenian women received no education whatever. (For an Athenian girl to spend time listening to a Sophist make grammatical distinctions would have been inconceivable.) Accordingly, there was very little that a girl knew or could be entertaining about. In such conditions a union with such a person could only have been for the lowliest of reasons. (We can now appreciate how revolutionary Socrates' view about the equality of the sexes—*Republic*, Book V—must have appeared.) Socrates would have made the moral distinction, but not the same one as Pausanias'.

ERYXIMACHUS (185 C): Eryximachus is the reserved physician, giving a medical theory of love. In the context of the celebration, such a learned disquisition has a dry humor about it. His talk also serves to raise the level of the discussion. He is saying, in effect, "Now that you mention good and bad love, you can find the good and bad elsewhere in the cosmos, you know, not only in man. As a matter of fact, there are opposites everywhere. In the human body, we find good and bad 'humors' which the physician must reconcile. Another set of opposites is the constant build-up and break-down that is going on—metabolism and katabolism. And in the cosmos as well, you find the opposed poles of hot and cold, wet and dry, and so on."

ARISTOPHANES (189 A): This is the famous comic playwright. We expect him to be funny, and he is—with one of the most famous sections in all the dialogues. Aristophanes knocks into a cocked hat all the cosmological razzle-dazzle we have heard so far. He offers a creation-myth of his own: before humans were as they are now, he says, they were combined into monsters that were each of them two people, back to back, one head with two faces. They had four legs and four arms. There were three combinations of sexes: male-male, female-female, and male-female. They were so powerful that Zeus split them in half. And ever since, each of us has been looking for his missing half to make him complete. Men who were once part of a male-female monster fall in love with women and the others look for their counterparts. But we must take care not to become too high-and-mighty, or Zeus will split us again, and we will all be hopping around on one leg and with half a face. (As to the imagery of the monster, doesn't Shakespeare characterize the sexual act as "the two-backed beast"? There is, however, a serious point in Socrates' presentation for which Aristophanes has prepared the groundwork: love is a state of incompleteness. What it will take to complete it—that is precisely the point at issue!)

AGATHON (194 E):   Agathon's speech is what you would expect from a recent award-winner in drama: a construction that is artificial, abstract, fanciful and with little relation to reality. This is important for the dialogue, however, because Socrates' mysticism will seem realistic by comparison. Eros is the most beautiful of the gods, Agathon says, and then he describes the god's qualities on the basis of certain analogies (the god is young, soft, etc.). Further, Eros has all the virtues, and these also are demonstrated on a vague basis of analogy. For example, the god has justice, for he neither does wrong nor suffers it; he has courage, temperance, and wisdom—for reasons that we can see are equally far-fetched. It is all very high-blown, and ends in a string of adjectives that overwhelm us with their emptiness and triviality (197 E).

SOCRATES (199 C):   Socrates begins by questioning Agathon, and the aim is to explode all this mythology. Love, Socrates shows us (how wisely!), is *not* a positive state nor a fixed condition to which we can ascribe certain properties (as Agathon had done). Rather, it is a condition of change and process. When we desire, it is always what we do not yet have. If love is the desire for beauty, then love cannot *be* beauty or *have* beauty. The idea that love is a process rather than a fixed state will be highly important to Socrates. He will describe love in terms of the soul's journey, its ascent to the limits of mystic vision. The words will be presented as those of a priestess who taught Socrates the mysteries when he was young. Her name is Diotima of Mantinea. We may ask why Plato has Socrates use this indirect method of presentation? The answer is that Socrates is to speak about that which cannot be uttered. It can only be pointed to, indirectly.

SOCRATES AND DIOTIMA (201 D):   The language used here is that which became traditional for whole centuries of mystics, visionaries and ecstatics—whether Buddhist, or Hindu, Christian or Jewish. What is being described by Diotima is the journey of the soul from the immediate experience of the day-to-day world up to a realm beyond time. It is the prisoner crawling out of the cave (see the *Republic*, Book VII). It is the climb up the scale of reality (see the Divided Line, the *Republic*, Book VI), from the illusory "realities" of our ordinary existence up to a glimpse of the supreme reality which is timeless and has no part in change. Diotima is shown to repeat what Socrates said earlier in talking to Agathon: the soul in love is not yet good, not yet beautiful, not yet wise. But this does not mean that it is evil, or ugly or ignorant. It is somewhere between, or else it would not be in transit (somewhere between B1 and A2, let us say, using the Divided Line of the *Republic*, Book VI).

The essence of love is uncertainty and process. In the same way, we may say that Eros is not a god nor a mortal, but something between the two—a spirit, taking men's prayers up to the gods and bringing the gods' revelations down to men. (Contrast all this with the speech of Phaedrus at the start of our dialogue, and see how far we have come: we have raised love to the level at which it becomes the symbol of divine communion.) Love is a way, also, of yearning for eternity. The lower type of love perpetuates itself in physical offspring, and grasps at eternity that way. But the birth of ideas is more enduring. This is made clear in the soul's ascent.

Diotima describes the exact stages of the soul's ascent (210 D): from its earliest recognition of physical beauty to beauty of thought, to a recognition of the underlying relation between all physical beauty to a love of all forms, to a realization that beauty of soul is still higher, to a recognition of the beauty in institutions and laws, to the beauties of science, and then up to the final vision of beauty alone, in and for itself—a vision of a unified understanding, a single science which is *also* the science of the beauty in all things! The road for this journey is beauty. Thus, we learn to go from beautiful individuals to the beauty of forms in general, and from these to beautiful practices, to beautiful concepts, to the essence of absolute beauty. And it is *this*, then, that is the genuine immortality!

ALCIBIADES (212 C):   Why does Plato introduce Alcibiades here, after Socrates has spoken? It is to make the contrast complete between the visionary Socrates and a man fully immersed in the temporal world. This contrast with Alcibiades will make Socrates' withdrawal from this dying world even more remote and sane. Alcibiades is at the height of his power as the leader of the upcoming Athenian expedition against Syracuse. (See A. E. Taylor's ingenious way of dating the dialogue, in his *Plato: The Man and His Work*.) Alcibiades describes his early admiration for Socrates, stemming from the time when Alcibiades as a young man tried to seduce the older Socrates, but with no success. Alcibiades' passion only increased. He describes how he fought alongside Socrates at the battle of Potidaea, and what a valiant fighter and robust drinker Socrates was—always in control, never drunk (drunkenness is what people whose souls are in disorder—who can't handle their problems—suffer from), and yet out-drinking everybody. Thus, the description already tells us much about the preparation for the mystic way! It is this gifted Alcibiades (who, at the time of the dialogue, is at the top of the political and military world) who now admits that the life of reason, the life of the mystic way, would have been better! (216 A). That is the point of having him here: he acts as a kind of closing testimonial to what Socrates had said about the truest kind of life.

Alcibiades' description also includes testimony of Socrates' extraordinary powers of enduring cold and hunger. There are references as well (220 C) to a 24-hour trance during the time of the military expedition. This brings the dialogue to a neat circle since it is the same kind of mystic trance with which the dialogue began.

The dialogue closes, however, on a subtle piece of irony: at daybreak, only Socrates, Aristophanes and Agathon are still awake, and Socrates is making the point that the true artist in tragedy ought to be capable of being an artist in comedy as well. When Aristophanes and Agathon fall asleep, Socrates leaves for the baths and is ready for another day. Why is this point made, and why here? The answer, perhaps, is this: poetry, too, is a kind of vision, a madness (see the *Phaedrus*). If a man could be a *true* artist and could reduce his art to definite principles, he could be as competent in one form of writing as another. But no artist can elaborate such principles—and that is Socrates' basis for condemning poets in the *Republic*, as we saw. Had the two men stayed awake, Socrates would no doubt have enlarged upon this theme—to show that poetry is not art but mysticism, and a low level of mysticism, at that. But the two poets have collapsed, and are deprived of even this articulated insight. The provocative problem of tragedy and comedy as art is enclosed in a phrase that is merely wafted in during the last ten lines of our dialogue, and is left hovering without an answer. The dialogue, therefore is incomplete—as is most every other dialogue. But that is as it should be, after all, because love is merely a process of becoming wise; it is not yet wisdom.

APOLOGY

INTRODUCTION: The *Apology*, the *Crito* and the *Phaedo* are the dialogues which deal directly with Socrates' trial and death. In the scene of the trial, it is apparent that Socrates is consciously choosing death. His defense (so-called) consists largely in showing how the prejudices against him have arisen, and how he has the highest possible justification for the life he has led (the command of God). This is obviously a very arrogant tone to take when one is on trial for one's life. But Socrates not only adopts this dangerous tone, he surpasses it.

THE CHARGES: Socrates is accused of corrupting the young, of disbelieving in the gods of the state and of introducing new deities. These charges can be understood in light of the historical situation: under the act of amnesty following the defeat of Athens in 404 B.C., no man could be tried for war crimes or for acts committed during the war. Accordingly, the accusers of Socrates could not very well say, "It is you and intellectuals like you that undermined the loyalties of the young and lost us the war." This is the real charge behind all this. But since this could not be said, the charge had to be worded as vaguely as possible.

Further, the notorious Alcibiades who betrayed the Athenians and defected to the Spartan side—and then sold out both to the arch-enemy of all Greeks: the Persian Empire—had been, as we saw, a young friend of Socrates. Had not Alcibiades been influenced by Socrates? Is not the teacher responsible? It is this sort of thing that the accusers intended the court to have in mind when the charge was "corruption of the young." The charge of impiety, likewise, indirectly refers to certain acts of desecration and profanation of the holy mysteries committed by Alcibiades (he disguised himself as a woman and attended rites which only women could witness; see any good history on this). Socrates is being held responsible for the impieties of his "followers"—but because of the amnesty the indictment must be indefinite. This explains Meletus' stammering performance.

Socrates undertakes to question his accuser in order to clarify the charges. But Meletus is hamstrung by the fact that he cannot make his charges explicit without risking a mistrial. Socrates knows this and presses him to the wall: By the charge of disbelief in the gods you mean I am an atheist? Yes. And an atheist believes there are no gods? Yes. Then how can I teach strange gods, as it says in the indictment, if I do not believe in gods at all?

THE DEFENSE: Socrates begins by explaining how the early prejudices against him arose. He was lampooned in the theater (chiefly in Aristophanes' play, *The Clouds*). In addition, there has been this habit of consistently questioning all he met. The reason for this constant questioning is a mysterious utterance by the oracle of the god Apollo at Delphi. The oracle had said that Socrates was the wisest of men. Socrates felt that this could not be true since he knew how ignorant he was. So he set about to disprove the oracle. He looked for someone wiser than himself. He examined the politicians, then the poets and playwrights and finally the artisans. None of them had any articulated scientific knowledge to support their actions. And he tried to show them that they did not "know" what they were doing. In pursuing this quest, Socrates had offended many powerful people. But the oracle was proved correct—although in a very oblique sense: the oracle, who always speaks in riddles, intended to say, "Only God is wise. Socrates is the smartest of men and that is only because he alone knows that his wisdom is nothing."

In addition to this, Socrates felt that God had given to him specifically the mission of "searching into myself and other men"—and that if he were offered the choice either of being set free on the condition that he would never do this again or else of being put to death, he must choose to heed the command of God. I shall not change my ways, Socrates says. The state is a great lazy horse, and I am the gadfly that stings it to activity. God has put me here for this purpose. "I believe that no greater good has ever happened in the state than my service to the God" (30 A).

THE JUDGMENT: In modern courts, only the jury can decide on questions of fact and only the judge can decide on questions of law. In the trial of Socrates, there are no judges and juries in the modern sense. The court is an assembly of 500 who are both judges of fact and of law. (There is no appeal.) The verdict is against Socrates, 280 to 220. Now he has to propose a penalty. The accusers had asked for the death penalty. Socrates refuses to suggest imprisonment or exile, since he has done no wrong. He suggests that if he were to get his due he should be put up at the house for visiting dignitaries—since he is the state's greatest benefactor. He says this after he has already been pronounced guilty. This is the point at which anyone else would have pleaded for mercy, with assurances that he would change his ways. But Socrates insists that he would never change his way of life; he must continue his questioning. "The unexamined life is not worth living." (38 A).

CRITO

The scene is in prison, about thirty days later. Crito brings word that Socrates must die within a few days unless he consents to escape. Sympathy will be on his side, because he was condemned unjustly. Socrates answers, however, that the decision was perfectly legal even though it was unjust. A good citizen must submit to the law. He cannot go against its decisions anytime the law does not suit him—or there would be an end to law. (It should be pointed out that this is no empty conformity on his part—not in a man who is society's severest critic. Whenever we hear the language of conformity it is always from people outside prison, so to speak. If Socrates is willing to conform, and pay for that conformity with his life, he must have a reason that is different from the usual argument for conformity.)

Crito appeals to him by saying that his friends will be disgraced for letting Socrates die. But that will only be the opinion of the many, Socrates says, and that does not matter. Yet it does matter, Crito insists, since it is their opinion that has put you here. Yes, responds Socrates, but the many cannot make a man wise or foolish, and that is what counts. Let us ignore their opinion.

We do not ask the many about a judgment in medicine. We can only go to someone with expert knowledge. Yet, the many are powerful, and can put me to death. But the most important thing is not life, merely, but the good life, the right life. Would it be *right* to escape? No, not if by having lived all my life in this city I have given my tacit consent to the system of things. Can I throw off the entire system merely because it now goes against me? A fine lot of talk my defense would seem, then: all that talk about having a mission in the state, and so on. If I went to another place my own hypocrisy would be thrown at me the moment I got into an argument, and rightly so! No, there is nothing to do but act in good faith. And let the consequences fall as they may. Justice first, then considerations of family and friends.

Socrates pretends that the laws are coming to talk to him. They say to him that he has had an agreement with them, all his life, to abide by their word. Any escape would be an attack against the laws themselves, and how can such an attack be justified in the present instance? They (together with customs and mores) have given him his way of life. He must not attack the entire system (with which he is in agreement) because of one law that is not in his interest. This is the voice he hears in his ears, he says, and it drowns out any other.

PHAEDO

INTRODUCTION: In the *Protagoras*, as we saw, the simple question "Can virtue be taught?" carries with it a whole cluster of questions that are most important for the human sciences as a whole. Here in the *Phaedo*, the question seems to be: "Is the soul immortal?" But the implications are much more far-reaching than this. Is the soul in touch with eternal reality? Can it have ultimate knowledge? Is it reducible to bodily functions? In other words, is the soul divine so that it is worth a lifetime of concern and careful tending? Thus, the dialogue serves to justify Socrates in his whole way of life. It is only because the soul is divine that it merits this pre-eminent attention; it is only because the soul is the divine in us that we are asked to avoid the life of *careless* sensuality or *empty* ambition, for it is these things that rivet the soul to the body.

It is the last day of Socrates' life. The chains have been taken off his legs. His wife and children have been to see him and then have been sent home. He rubs his leg where the shackle was, and he makes a remark about how pain and pleasure are inevitably tied together. This would ordinarily be the perfect opener for one of his familiar discussions about the relation between pain and pleasure. But he cannot take the time for this now. It is his last day on earth, and he must get on to the more pressing question of whether he will survive his death at sunset. (None of my enemies can say now that I talk about matters that are none of my business, he says.)

PHILOSOPHY AND DEATH: The pleasure-pain theme leads naturally into a very powerful idea. Socrates remarks that Aesop should have composed a fable about pleasure and pain. Now that we're on the subject of writers and poets, Cebes says, I have been asked by a poet why you, Socrates, who have never written a line, have been spending your time in here making verses out of Aesop's fables. Socrates says that in the course of his life he has had a recurring dream telling him to "make music." He had always interpreted this dream to mean that he should pursue philosophy (the soul's harmony). But just in case the dream is intended to be taken literally, he has composed actual music.

In any case, he says, tell the poet not to worry about my poetry, but rather to come after me if he has any sense. It is not likely that he will, Cebes says. Why, asks Socrates, is he not a philosopher? *All philosophy is a rehearsal for death!* Here, Socrates puts his legs off the couch, thereby emphasizing the fact that he is making an important point. Suicide is wrong. (As, in the *Crito*, he refused to escape from prison, so he will not take the means to make his own escape from his body.) The gods are our guardians and we cannot run out on them. Why, then, should a philosopher be anxious to leave this life?

Socrates is convinced that he is going to a world of other gods, better men. But he must defend this idea of immortality. In court, he lost the battle for the life of his body; here he is fighting for the life of his soul. A warning comes from the attendant that Socrates must not talk too much and get overheated or the poison may not work effectively and he may have to take more. Then I shall take more, Socrates says—another dramatic symbol for the idea that he is willing to undergo many trials for the sake of getting at the truth.

THE REVERSAL OF VALUES: Now, what about the idea that the philosopher rehearses for death, and pursues it? This involves a reversal of values: people in the ordinary run of experience hold that dying is a process going from life to the absence of life. They are right to feel bad about it. But for a philosopher, death is a process from death to life: this world is already a death, this body is a prison. Accordingly, death is a release, a liberation, a process that is positive. (This reversal of values is typical of many great moralists. St. Augustine says, "I know not how I came into this, shall I call it a dying life or a living death?")

Death is the separation of soul from body. And philosophers have all during their lives tried to get to the soul as it really is, apart from its imprisonment in the body. They have tried to see the truth with the eye of the mind, not with the body's eyes.

Our bodily senses tell us only about particulars. Only thought can tell us of universals. As philosophers, what we have been trying to do all our lives is to separate our soul's activities from our body's. Now that the real separation of soul from body is to take place, and we are getting that which we have been struggling for, ought we not to rejoice? The question remains, however, as Cebes points out, whether the soul lives on after the separation.

FIRST ARGUMENT FOR IMMORTALITY: CYCLE AND RECOL-LECTION (70 C): It is my view that the first and second arguments are not intended as "proofs," or as representing the final views of Socrates—but rather that they are offered as speculations in the light of the then current views of science, religion and morality. Thus, these "arguments" are offered so that they might have their weaknesses exposed. When they are overthrown, we are ready for Socrates' proof in the third argument.

The first argument contains two elements: the cycle theory and the recollection theory. As we shall see, they must go together in order to make a complete argument. The cycle theory says that in all of nature there is a constant process of alternation: night-day-night . . . summer-winter-summer . . . waking-sleeping-waking . . . . Can we not say that there is a cycle of life-death-life-death, etc.? Or could nature walk on one leg only? If there were one process only, then everything would ultimately come to an end. Still, the cycle theory does not prove that there is a persistence of identity, it shows merely that *some* sort of life recurs. It is no comfort to me to think that I might return without my identity, or in another form of life. What sort of immortality is that? The soul must be more than an innocuous piece of cyclical nature. Socrates therefore augments the cycle theory with the theory of recollection.

Even though Socrates made frequent use of the theory of recollection (see the *Meno*) it is not original with him, but perhaps goes back to the Pythagoreans. The *Meno*, it will be recollected, spoke of the theory of recollection in the light of the way we can bring out from within ourselves mathematical knowledge we could not have learned in this lifetime. Perhaps the soul pre-existed, and learned these truths in a former life. Certainly, if these ideas can be said to have existed before we were born, then it follows that our souls must have pre-existed also, "and if not the ideas, then not the souls." (76 E). This would imply a persistence of identity (although only dimly retained).

But this proves only that the soul existed before this life; it does not follow that the soul will continue after this life. Now if there is a former experience (as the recollection theory tells us), and there is also a present experience (as is obvious), then if we add the cycle theory to this, the process will be completed by an "after," and we shall have a perfect model for a theory of immortality that has a place for the retention of identity. Cebes is not convinced and wants another argument.

SECOND ARGUMENT FOR IMMORTALITY: DUALISM (78 B):
Socrates is here attempting to describe the soul as substance that is *simple*, not made up of different elements. Something which has no parts cannot fall to pieces. He is also trying to show that the soul is *immutable*. Something that cannot change, cannot be affected by circumstances—such as death. We have already seen in the Divided Line (the *Republic*, Book VI) how Socrates divides the world into the area that can be apprehended by the senses (B), and the area that can be apprehended only by intelligence (A). Visible things (B) undergo change—chairs fall apart. The ideas (A) never change: $a^2 + b^2 = c^2$.

Now, to which group does the body belong, and to which the soul? Clearly, the body has organs that put it in touch with the sensory world; such is the only kind of reality which the body can know. Further, the body itself is visible and undergoes change, so it obviously belongs to (B). But the soul, we know, understands ideas directly, and tries not to rely on the senses at all. The reality it grasps is unchanging. Further, the soul is invisible, so that it must belong to (A). Presumably, too, it must be immutable, incapable of being changed, unaffected by what happens to the body (even at the body's death), and is therefore immortal.

> **COMMENT:** The presumption made by Socrates is the idea that all reality comes in two kinds: the sensory (B) and the intelligible (A). It is a safe bet that if a man is a powerful moralist, he is a dualist also. He tends to see the world in a series of opposing pairs: mind *vs.* matter, reason *vs.* sensation, light *vs.* darkness, good *vs.* evil, eternity

vs. time, body *vs.* soul, etc. His outlook is such that he sees dualisms everywhere. (The weakness of any dualism is this: one element is always less real than the other. This means that a dualism inevitably ends by distrusting some area of our experience—body is not as real as soul, etc.— because each is of a different *value*. A dualistic universe is one that makes a place for values.)

Modern scientists, however, are anything but dualists, and that is because they want to see nature as morally neutral, stripped of values. Thus, they want nothing but the facts. Good and evil are not facts, they are values. Because scientists need no values in nature, they need no dualisms. There is no "*vs.*" in nature, as far as they are concerned. Everything is nothing but particles in motion, or nothing but quanta of energy, etc. Scientists, therefore, are by nature *monistic*—meaning that they find *one* kind of substance or quality underlying all their reality—not dualistic.

OBJECTIONS TO SOCRATES' ARGUMENTS (85 C): Simmias and Cebes, speaking for the science of their time, make monistic objections to Socrates' dualism. Simmias is what is now called an "epiphenomenalist"—he sees the soul as nothing but an effect of the body. The soul (psychological behavior) is nothing but bodily behavior (the ionization of neurons, etc.) so there is nothing but bodily behavior going on, and we may say that there is only *one* kind of reality in us: the physical. He compares body and soul to the lyre and the music it gives off. If the soul is the body's "music," then once the instrument dies we cannot say that the music lives on. If the instrument is broken, then no further music can be expected from it. Thus, the body outlasts the soul, as the lyre outlasts the music—and there is no immortality for the soul.

Cebes' position is now called "mechanism." He says that we may regard the soul as that which operates the body, and that which "makes" the body by controlling metabolism, and so on. His position is the opposite of Simmias'. For Simmias, soul is the effect of body. For Cebes, the body is an effect of the soul. But for both men, there is no immortality. Cebes compares soul and body to a weaver who weaves many cloaks. We make many bodies in one lifetime—all our cells are replaced in seven years. A seventy-year-old man would have used up ten bodies. The last cloak the weaver makes (his last "body") outlasts him. Here too, then, the body outlasts the soul and there is no immortality.

> **COMMENT:** This is a very telling point that Plato is making. There are many reasons why he presents the objections of Simmias and Cebes as he does. But I believe that Plato's main point (as author of the dialogue) is to show us that as soon as we take a scientific, monistic view, and reduce soul to a kind of bodily function or reduce body to the soul's activity, all immortality and all morality are rejected. (Obviously, Behaviorism has nothing to say about moral questions.) Socrates will show us the most damaging weaknesses of the scientific approach. First, however, he will reply to the objections.

SOCRATES' REPLY TO THE OBJECTIONS (91 C):   Simmias had accepted the theory of recollection, but he also believes that the soul is merely the "music" of the body. But these two ideas are incompatible: epiphenomenalism says that the soul is an effect of the body, so it cannot exist before the body, any more than the lyre's music can exist before the lyre does; yet the recollection theory says the soul did pre-exist. Further, if the analogy of the lyre held true, that the soul were a music or harmony of the body, then better attuned souls would be more of a harmony and therefore more real as souls. But all souls—good or bad, healthy or sick—are equally real. And if we had to say that their moral "attunement" is the same, then there can be no moral differences between individuals. Yet we know there are such differences. Thus, Socrates needs dualism in order to allow for the obvious moral differences between people. And thus, epiphenomenalism overlooks this difference and thereby clashes with reality. (Note: In the *Republic*, Socrates speaks of the soul as a harmony, but it is not a harmony of the body.)

As to Cebes' objection, mechanism says that the life processes of the body—metabolism and katabolism—eventually wear out the soul. We must therefore ask whether this mechanistic analogy can be applied at all.

> **MECHANISM VERSUS TELEOLOGY:** This has become a classic problem in philosophy. (This is discussed more fully in the Monarch books on Hegel and on Kant.) Mechanism explains nature in terms of causes that come before the event. In answer to the question, "Why is there a

wind?" we can say: "Winds are produced by a previous change in air pressures, which are produced by prior changes in air temperature, which come about because there is an earlier change from light to dark as the earth rotates." Science seeks to explain everything mechanistically, but in terms of *prior* causes. But what this excludes is any kind of purpose or value or goal.

But if we did not know what *prior* forces had brought the wind into being, we might seek an explanation in terms of factors coming *after* the event, such factors as purposes or goals. (The Greek word for "goal" or "end" is *telos*— hence "teleology": explaining something in terms of its uses or purposes, not in terms of its origins.) In answer to the question, "Why is there a wind?" we might say: "Winds are there so that we can have sailboats and windmills and cool summers." (The example is purposely trivial, to make it clear. We do say, in zoology, "The anteater has a long snout so that he can get into the ant hills . . . the zebra, etc.") In a mechanistic explanation, a thing can best be explained by what went before. In a teleological explanation, a thing can best be explained by what comes after.

SOCRATES AND ALL THIS: It is possible to show that scientific, mechanistic explanations are *largely* inapplicable to life-situations. If I ask, "How is it that that man is shouting, 'Help'?" a teleologist would explain (in terms of events coming *after*) that the man is drowning and wants to attract our attention; a mechanist would explain (in terms of events immediately *prior*, as an expert behaviorist observer would do) that the man is uttering this sound as the result of opening his mouth in a certain characteristic shape, putting his tongue over his lower teeth, filling his lungs with air (those parts not already filled with water), etc.

To show that mechanism is inapplicable (and thus to answer Cebes), Socrates recounts his own enthusiasm for the early scientists who promised to explain everything. What they did not explain is the teleological *Why*. A mechanistic explanation of why I am here, he says, would describe my posture on this couch, the arrangement of my bones and sinews, and so on— hardly an adequate explanation. But a teleological explanation of my being here would say that I am awaiting death at the hands of my fellow-citizens. (This conflict between the two types of explanation, and the question of which is the more adequate to the human sciences, is now a burning issue. The one is more scientific—corresponding to physics as a model; the other "explains" better.)

THIRD PROOF OF IMMORTALITY (102 A):   We can call a certain man shorter than Mr. X and taller than Mr. Y. But this does not mean that our man is both short and tall in the sense in which these contradict one another. If the terms are relative, and we use them only in saying "shorter than," "taller than," then all is well. But we cannot speak of a "tall short man." And the reason why we cannot call a man a "tall short man," or speak of a "circular square" is that the adjectives partake of different forms.

As we saw in the Divided Line (the *Republic*, Book VI), forms are eternal ideas which all particular sensible things imitate. Now, the reason why there cannot *be* a "tall short man" is that no particular thing can imitate two contradictory forms. Socrates piles up endless examples, but the point can be made simply. When a thing is a circle, it "partakes of," or "participates in," or "imitates" the form of circularity. If it partakes of squareness it ceases to *be* a circle precisely because it ceases to partake of circularity.

Now, the form that the soul partakes of is life. Therefore a soul could not possibly partake of death. If it did, it would either cease to be a soul or cease to be. Thus, we can never predicate the property word "dead" of a soul any more than we can describe a circle by calling it square.

The soul does not partake of death and cannot do so. Therefore, when the body dies, the soul must retire, withdraw. It itself cannot suffer death and still be called a soul! This concept can be understood only in the light of the *reality* of forms. They are not merely mental contents, but the most real of things, so that their visible counterparts are mere imitations.

CONCLUSION: Socrates has shown that a life of virtue *is* a meaningful program: if the world is to be understood as rational, then there must be forms to account for that rationality; and if we admit the forms, then we must admit the souls—

as he suggests earlier (76 E). To give allegorical scope to all this, the talk by this man waiting to die turns to a mythical description of the earth and a vision of judgment after death. The aim, as was said, is to demonstrate the underlying rationality in the world that makes a rational life possible. It is this alone that has made it a sensible thing to spend one's life in care for the soul.

The dialogue now ends with the death of Socrates and is as dramatic and powerful as one would expect.

ESSAY QUESTIONS AND ANSWERS

1. What is the problem about justice with which Socrates is confronted at the beginning of the *Republic*?

ANSWER: In Book I, Thrasymachus presents the argument that "justice is the interest of the stronger"; that is, justice is whatever the power-structure of a society says it is. If the ruler is a tyrant, then he defines "justice" as that which serves *his* interests. If the state is a democracy, then it defines "justice" as that which is approved of by the majority. Thus, justice is relative to the political environment in which it is found. There are no higher laws, no "absolute" justice, by which any actual form of justice can be judged as being good or bad. The shepherd, Thrasymachus says, raises his sheep for his own interest, not for theirs.

In Book II, Glaucon seems to confirm the idea that justice is the interest of the stronger. He presents us with a myth in which a man has the power to make himself invisible. This gives him absolute power to do as he likes. Now, if we give this power to the unjust man as well as to the just man, we shall find (Glaucon says) that their actions are identical. This shows that the only apparent difference between the unjust man and the just man is that the former has power and the latter does not; but give the just man this power and he becomes totally unjust. Men create moral codes because they are weak, and want to protect themselves against the strong.

It is Socrates' aim (throughout the remainder of the *Republic*) to show that injustice is a disease, in the individual as in the state. If a man or state were truly "healthy," with all parts integrated in a harmony, then that man or state would not commit injustice, even if given the power to do so.

2. What is Socrates' view of the relation between politics and psychology, in the *Republic*?

ANSWER: Socrates analyzes the individual soul into its faculties. Then he magnifies this picture of the soul, dealing with it
as though it were a political state. In this way, he can draw
continuous analogies between the individual soul and the state
and he can see the same forces at work in both. Thus, justice is
the same for the soul as for the state—so that politics is nothing but an extension, a magnification of psychology.

Corresponding to the faculties of reason, spirit and appetite in
the individual soul, Socrates posits the rulers (or guardians),
the soldiers and executives (or auxiliaries), and the populace.
What makes the analogy conclusive for Socrates is that the
same virtues apply to the faculties in the soul as to the parts of
the state. Thus, wisdom is the virtue controlling the correct use
of reason by the soul; wisdom is also the quality needed by the
guardians in the state. Courage is the virtue controlling the correct use of spirit by the soul; courage is also the quality needed
by the auxiliaries in the state. Temperance is the virtue controlling the correct use of appetites by the soul; temperance is
also the quality needed by the populace in the state. When
these functions are properly harmonized, each part doing its
own work and no other, we have justice in the state, as in the
soul.

3. What is the relation of thought to reality in the Theory of
Forms and the Divided Line as described in *Republic* VI?

ANSWER: The Theory of Forms (also called the Theory of
Ideas) attempts to account for the rationality of the world. The
world is rational, and can be known by science, only because
both the world *and* our thoughts participate in certain forms.
The device which Plato uses in order to explain this is the
Divided Line. The problem is this: We know that our ordinary
experience of the world gives us a contact *only* with individual
things. We see only this tree and this cat. We cannot, however,
have a science of particulars, that is, a science of *this* tree.
There can be only a science of trees in general. Yet, we can
have contact only with this one, not with generalities. How,
then, can we extract from our contact with individuals a concept that applies to all?

The answer is that we cannot do this with the senses. In order
to arrive at a concept, we must resort to a different psychological faculty: either understanding or reason. Further, the idea of

trees is more real than the particular tree, since the particular tree merely reflects the general idea. Accordingly, as we ascend up the scale of knowledge, from contact with particulars to a grasp of ideas, we also ascend up the scale of reality. The Divided Line is demarcated into two basic kinds of reality: the intelligible world and the sensible world. These are further subdivided so that the intelligible world contains pure ideas and those ideas requiring "visual aid," such as those of geometry. The sensible world is subdivided into particular objects and mere "reflections" of those particulars in mirages, shadows and reflections in mirrors, and so on. Thus as the reflections are not as real as the objects, so the objects are not as real as the ideas of them.

4. What is the Theory of Recollection in the *Meno*?

ANSWER: This is merely a symbolic representation, or analogy, about the capacity of the mind to know pure ideas. Socrates asks questions of a slave who has had no formal education in geometry. By asking certain questions, Socrates is able to extract the correct answers from the slave. How is this evident knowledge of the slave to be explained? He did not gain this knowledge from his experience. Obviously, he already had the ideas "within" him. But this, too, is an unsatisfactory explanation. If we say he was born with these "innate" (inborn) ideas, this still does not account for the validity of these ideas, nor how he came to have them. Socrates concludes with the inference that the slave must have known these ideas before he was born, and is now only slowly being made to "recollect" them. It must be stressed that Socrates does not take this literally. He uses the concept of "recollection" only as a symbolic justification for the theory of ideas which we know by a capacity we all have "within" us.

5. In the *Protagoras*, what is Socrates' view on the question, "Can virtue be taught?"

ANSWER: Socrates' position in the beginning of the dialogue is that virtue cannot be taught, if we mean by "virtue" the conglomerate of conventional morality. This is passively taken in, the way we learn our mother-tongue. It is not taught, in the sense that the student comes to see the justification for it. Toward the end of the dialogue, however, he shows that we must re-define "virtue" as a set of fully rationalized, articulate principles. In this sense, only, can we say that virtue can be taught. Socrates bases this on the concept that virtue is knowledge—that *all* virtues are kinds of knowing. In order to show this, he argues that all virtues are basically one. A corollary of this theory is the view that "no man does evil knowingly." Underlying all behavior is the principle that whatever is done, is done for some ostensible good. That "good" might be a mistaken notion, but no man acts counter to what he believes— rightly or wrongly—is his interest. Thus, all wrong-doing is error.

6. What are the conclusions about knowledge in the *Theaetetus*?

ANSWER: The conclusions are entirely negative, the point of the dialogue is to show that our conventional definitions are inadequate. First, the identification of knowledge with sensation is discussed. The discussion follows the Divided Line in separating the intelligible from the sensible world. Mere seeing is not a kind of knowing. I can hear a foreign language perfectly without understanding a word of it. Can we therefore re-define knowledge as true opinion? No, because an opinion can be true without involving knowledge—as in the case of the jury that happens to come to a correct verdict, but on the basis of emotion, and so on. Ought we therefore to modify this definition to say that knowledge is a true opinion together with an explanation or analysis? No, because we can analyze a fact down to its elements without understanding the whole. With these conventional definitions out of the way—and they comprise some of the most "important" definitions of knowledge—the way is open to further clarification.

7. How does Socrates deal with the concept of love in the *Symposium*?

ANSWER: Socrates uses the language of "eros" for the purpose of describing the soul's ascent to mystic vision. The other speakers in the dialogue begin with a discussion of love on the lower physical plane. Gradually, the quality of the discussion is raised to the spiritual level—punctuated by Aristophanes' hilarious explanation of why love is a search for our "lost halves." For Socrates, love is in an intermediate stage between ignorance and knowledge. It is its intermediate situation that accounts for love's striving to advance and attain its goal.

Through the teaching of a priestess, Diotima, we are told of the soul's striving to attain the vision of the good. The soul passes through stages of enlightenment beginning with the recognition of beauty in particulars and ending with a direct intuition of beauty in itself. Thus, love and mysticism are combined to represent both our desire to know as well as the highest goal which that knowing can attain.

8. How does Socrates overcome the "scientific" objections against the concept of immortality in the *Phaedo*?

ANSWER: Simmias contends that the soul is nothing but an effect of the body—meaning that psychological behavior is ultimately reducible to physiological descriptions. The analogy used is that the soul is the music made by the body which is an instrument. When the instrument is broken, there is no more music. Against this, Socrates points out that the soul is not merely an attunement of the body, for if this were true then a badly attuned soul would be less of a soul. Cebes objects that since the soul directs the growth and activities of the body, it must ultimately become worn out. The analogy used here is that the soul is a weaver who weaves many cloaks (bodies). After he weaves the last cloak, the weaver dies but the cloak remains. Socrates overcomes this by showing the inadequacy of all mechanistic interpretation in the human sciences. He describes his own intellectual development from the time he was interested in the speculations of the physicists. These thinkers sought to explain things in terms of their origins rather than in terms of their purposes. It can be shown that this latter type (teleological explanation) is the only one that is adequate for certain situations: the mechanistic explanation of his presence in the cell makes no sense, while the teleological explanation does: he is there awaiting death, and so on. Thus, the concept of immortality survives the attempt of science to reduce it to nothing.

BIBLIOGRAPHY

(*indicates that the book is available in paperback)

*E. Barker, *The Political Thought of Plato and Aristotle*, New York: Dover Press, 1959.

J. Burnet, *Greek Philosophy*, Part I, from Thales to Plato, London: Macmillan, 1920. (An important basic work.)

*F. Copleston, *A History of Philosophy*, Vol. I, Part 1, New York: Image Books, 1962. (Excellent.)

*F. M. Cornford, *From Religion to Philosophy*, New York: Harper, 1960.

*————, *Plato and Parmenides*, Indianapolis: Liberal Arts Press, (Plato's *Parmenides* and Parmenides' way of truth, together with running commentary.)

*————, *Plato's Theory of Knowledge*, Indianapolis: Liberal Arts Press. (A translation of the *Theaetetus* and the *Sophist* with running commentary.)

R. Demos, *The Philosophy of Plato*, Chicago: Scribner's, 1939.

G. C. Field, *The Philosophy of Plato*, Oxford: Home University Library, 1949.

*P. Friedländer, *Plato, An Introduction*, New York: Harper, 1962.

*W. K. C. Guthrie, *The Greek Philosophers*, New York: Harper, 1960.

W. Jaeger, *Paideia: The Ideals of Greek Culture*, 3 Vols., New York: Oxford University Press, 1945. (Excellent for its analysis of Plato and the cultural background.)

H. W. B. Joseph, *The Form of the Good in Plato's Republic*, London, 1948.

A. Koyre, *Discovering Plato*, New York, 1945.

*G. Murray, *Five Stages of Greek Religion*, New York: Doubleday, 1955.

R. L. Nettleship, *Lectures on the Republic of Plato*, London: Macmillan, 1898.

———, *The Theory of Education in Plato's Republic*, Oxford, 1935.

W. Pater, *Plato and Platonism*, New York, 1893.

D. Ross, *Plato's Theory of Ideas*, Oxford, 1957.

G. Santayana, *Platonism and the Spiritual Life*, New York: 1927.

*A. E. Taylor, *Plato*: *The Man and His Work*, New York: Meridian, 1957. (*The* indispensable analysis of the Dialogues.)

*———, *The Mind of Plato*, Ann Arbor, Michigan, 1960.

*———,*Socrates*, New York: Doubleday, 1953.

*W. Windelband, *A History of Philosophy*, Vol. I, New York: Harper, 1958.

E. Zeller, *Outlines of the History of Greek Philosophy*, London, 1931.